# WE CROSSED A BRIDGE AND IT TREMBLED

## VOICES FROM SYRIA

———

# WENDY PEARLMAN

HarperCollins books may be purchased for educational, business, or sales promotional use. For information please e-mail the Special Markets Department at SPsales@harpercollins.com.

A hardcover edition of this book was published in 2017 by Custom House, an imprint of William Morrow.

FIRST CUSTOM HOUSE PAPERBACK EDITION PUBLISHED 2018.

*Photo credit Muheisen/AP/REX/Shutterstock, Inc.*

Library of Congress Cataloging-in-Publication Data has been applied for.

ISBN 978-0-06-265444-1

19 20 21 22 LSC 10 9 8 7 6 5 4 3 2

## Praise for *We Crossed a Bridge and It Trembled*

"Everyone talks about Syrians, but very few actually talk to them. . . . *We Crossed a Bridge and It Trembled* bucks the trend. . . . These best of all possible informants—the people who made the events, and who suffer the consequences—provide not only gripping eyewitness accounts but erudite analysis and sober reflection. . . . The result is testament both to Syrian expressive powers and the translation's high literary standard. These heart-stopping tales of torment and triumph are perfectly enchained, chronologically and thematically, to reflect the course of the crisis." —*Guardian*

"I almost didn't open Wendy Pearlman's latest book. . . . But I was quickly hooked by Pearlman's simple and often captivating human narratives. . . . The momentum and unusual impact of this book are built by the wrenching candor of dozens of Syrians from all religions, ethnicities, and major cities. . . . The book does well to explain the challenges of the future, not only in ending the war but in healing a traumatized and shell-shocked society."

—*The New Yorker*

"This profoundly important book draws on hundreds of interviews to create an oral history of the Syrian uprising and the unfolding catastrophe that has followed. Pearlman, an accomplished political scientist, has chosen to let her Syrian interlocutors speak for themselves. What emerges is a complex, engaging and difficult oral history, which deserves a wide readership." —*Washington Post*

"The book is not a plea for pity but an invitation to empathy—to see Syrians as ordinary people, caught in a lethal vortex, forsaken by the world, but holding on to their humanity. Above all, the book is an assertion of memory against forgetting at a time when truth has become fragile." —*Times Literary Supplement*

"Equal parts heroic epic and tragedy, her book covers the events leading up to and following the Syrian uprising, stitching together the collective journey of Syrians to Jordan, Turkey, Lebanon, and countries throughout Europe. The result is a people's history of activists, mothers, doctors, students, actors, fighters, and therapists who describe life and loss during this tumultuous period."

—*Chicago* magazine

"Through the adroit combination of these voices, readers gain a solid grasp of the Syrian uprising and its deterioration into a bloody civil war from the point of view of participants and victims. . . . Pearlman masterfully intertwines the testimonies of her Syrian eyewitnesses to produce a rich chronological account." —Middle East Eye

"You may find yourself tearing through this grimly beautiful book in two sittings, giving it to people, wishing there were more of it. But on a policy level it will shake all your points of reference: humanitarianism, hard realism, and all the thoughtful dithering in between."

—Los Angeles Review of Books

"This book is something of a treasure trove, bustling with insight. In addition to giving Syrians a voice, it should be a companion to anything watched or read on Syria. It puts the very real, humanizing voices of Syrians back into the spotlight, which is precisely where they belong."

—New Arab

"A heartbreaking, human, and necessary book. Recommended for anyone who wishes to better understand the Syrian conflict." —*Library Journal*

# WE CROSSED A BRIDGE

# AND IT TREMBLED

## ALSO BY WENDY PEARLMAN

*Occupied Voices: Stories of Everyday Life from the Second Intifada*

*Violence, Nonviolence, and the Palestinian National Movement*

To those who did not live to complete their stories.

# Contents

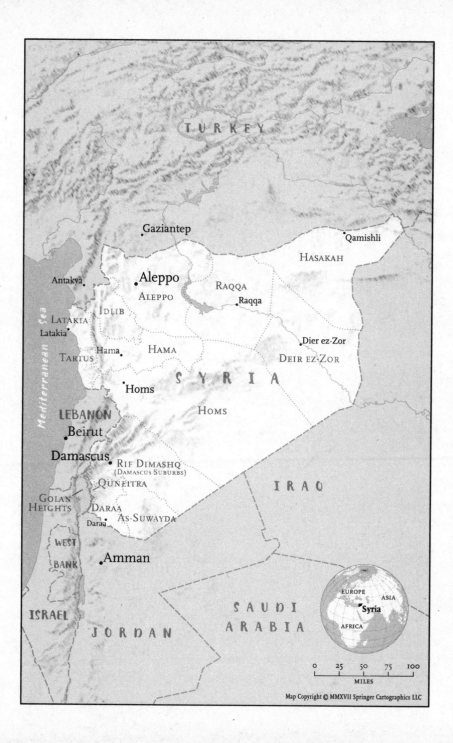

TURKEY

Gaziantep

Qamishli

HASAKAH

Antakya

Aleppo
ALEPPO

RAQQA
Raqqa

Latakia
LATAKIA
Latakia

IDLIB

Mediterranean Sea

Hama

HAMA

Dier ez-Zor
DEIR EZ-ZOR

TARTUS

Homs

S Y R I A

HOMS

LEBANON
Beirut

Damascus
RIF DIMASHQ
(DAMASCUS SUBURBS)

QUNEITRA

IRAQ

GOLAN
HEIGHTS

DARAA
Daraa

AS-SUWAYDA

WEST
BANK

Amman

ISRAEL

JORDAN

SAUDI
ARABIA

EUROPE      ASIA

Syria

AFRICA

0      25      50      75      100
MILES

Map Copyright © MMXVII Springer Cartographics LLC

# List of Speakers

**ABDEL-AZIZ**: French-language teacher from Sowura village in the Daraa Governorate. Interviewed in the Zaatari refugee camp, Jordan, on October 19, 2012.

**ABDEL-HALIM**: FSA fighter from Homs city. Interviewed in Gaziantep, Turkey, on January 10, 2016.

**ABDEL-NASER**: Financial manager and human rights activist from Douma in the Damascus suburbs. Interviewed in Stockholm, Sweden, on June 26, 2016.

**ABDEL-SAMED**: Business owner from al-Jeeza village in the Daraa Governorate. Interviewed in Irbid, Jordan, on September 17, 2012.

**ABDUL RAHMAN**: Engineer from Hama city. Interviewed in Copenhagen, Denmark, on June 14, 2016.

**ABED**: Defected military officer and FSA commander from Palmyra in the Homs Governorate. Interviewed in Amman, Jordan, on August 24, 2013.

**ABU FIRAS**: FSA fighter from Maarat al-Nu'man in the Idlib Governorate. Interviewed in Reyhanlı, Turkey, on September 20, 2013.

**ABU MA'AN**: Activist and FSA fighter from Daraa city. Interviewed in Amman, Jordan, on August 17, 2013, and by Skype from Irbid, Jordan, on November 15, 2013.

**ABU SAMIR**: Defected military officer and FSA commander from Douma in the Damascus suburbs. Interviewed in Antakya, Turkey, on September 1, 2013.

**ABU TAREK**: Engineer from a village in the Hama Governorate. Interviewed in Reyhanlı, Turkey, on September 25, 2013.

**ABU THA'IR**: Aeronautical engineer from Daraa city. Interviewed in Amman, Jordan, on September 16, 2012.

**ADAM**: Media organizer from Latakia city. Interviewed in Copenhagen, Denmark, on June 12, 2016.

**AHMED:** Activist from Daraa city. Interviewed in Amman, Jordan, on October 9, 2012, and by Skype from Leesburg, Virginia, on October 27, 2016, and November 27, 2016.

**AMAL:** Former university student from Aleppo city. Interviewed in Gaziantep, Turkey, on October 1, 2013.

**AMIN:** Physical therapist from Aleppo city. Interviewed in Gaziantep, Turkey, on January 10, 2016.

**ANNAS:** Doctor from Ghouta in the Damascus suburbs. Interviewed in Antakya, Turkey, on September 22, 2013.

**ASHRAF:** Artist from Qamishli in the Hasakah Governorate. Interviewed in Antakya, Turkey, on September 3, 2013.

**AYHAM:** Web developer from Damascus. Interviewed in Copenhagen, Denmark, on June 12, 2016.

**AZIZA:** School principal from Hama city. Interviewed in Dubai, United Arab Emirates, on March 20, 2016.

**BESHR:** Cinematography student from Damascus. Interviewed in Istanbul, Turkey, on March 22, 2016.

**BILLAL:** Doctor from Harasta in the Damascus suburbs. Interviewed in Chicago, Illinois, on May 20, 2016.

**BUSHRA:** Mother from al-Tel in the Damascus suburbs. Interviewed in an informal tent settlement in Marj, Bekaa Valley, Lebanon, on February 1, 2016.

**CAPTAIN:** FSA fighter from Aleppo city. Interviewed in Antakya, Turkey, on September 10, 2013.

**CHERIN:** Mother from Aleppo city. Interviewed in Antakya, Turkey, on September 3, 2013.

**EYAD:** Law school graduate from Daraya in the Damascus suburbs. Interviewed in Mörrum, Sweden, on June 20, 2016.

**FADI:** Theater set and lighting specialist from Hama city. Interviewed in Amman, Jordan, on September 20, 2012.

**FIRAS:** Computer engineer and journalist from Aleppo city. Interviewed in Gaziantep, Turkey, on January 9, 2016.

**FOUAD:** Surgeon from Aleppo city. Interviewed in Beirut, Lebanon, on January 29, 2016.

**GHASSAN:** Artist from the Khan al-Shih Palestinian refugee camp. Interviewed in Berlin, Germany, on June 22, 2016.

**GHAYTH:** Former university student in economics from Aleppo city. Interviewed in Berlin, Germany, on July 23, 2016.

**HADI:** Shop owner from Salma village in the Latakia Governorate. Interviewed in Antakya, Turkey, on September 7, 2013.

**HADIA:** Clinical therapist from Damascus. Interviewed in Chicago, Illinois, on May 20, 2016.

**HAKEM:** Agricultural engineer and pharmacist from Deir ez-Zor. Interviewed in Berlin, Germany, on July 24, 2016.

**HAMOUDI:** Engineering graduate from Aleppo city. Interviewed in Antakya, Turkey, on September 4, 2013.

**HANEEN:** University graduate from Daraya in the Damascus suburbs. Interviewed in a village near Kiel, Germany, on June 11, 2016.

**HIBA:** Former university student in pharmacy from Qalamoun in the Damascus suburbs. Interviewed in Beirut, Lebanon, on January 30, 2016.

**HOSAM:** Computer programmer from al-Tel in the Damascus suburbs. Interviewed in Amman, Jordan, on October 16, 2012.

**HUSAYN:** Playwright from Aleppo city. Interviewed in Gaziantep, Turkey, on January 11, 2016.

**IBRAHIM:** Former university student in computer science from a village in the Hama Governorate. Interviewed in Reyhanlı, Turkey, on September 25, 2013.

**ILIYAS:** Dentist from Skalbiya village in the Hama Governorate. Interviewed in Antakya, Turkey, on September 5, 2013.

**IMAD:** Former university student from Salamiyah. Interviewed in Berlin, Germany, on August 2, 2016.

**IMAN:** Engineer from Harasta in the Damascus suburbs. Interviewed in Chicago, Illinois, on May 20, 2016.

**ISSAM:** Accountant from a village in the Aleppo Governorate. Interviewed in Istanbul, Turkey, on November 12, 2015.

**JALAL:** Photographer from Aleppo city. Interviewed in Gaziantep, Turkey, on January 10, 2016.

**JAMAL:** Doctor from Hama city. Interviewed in Irbid, Jordan, on October 11, 2012.

**KAREEM:** Doctor from Homs city. Interviewed in Amman, Jordan, on August 26, 2013, and Berlin, Germany, on July 2, 2016.

**KHALIL:** Defected military officer and FSA commander from Deir ez-Zor city. Interviewed in Antakya, Turkey, on September 21, 2013.

**KINDA:** Activist from Suwayda city. Interviewed in Gaziantep, Turkey, on October 4, 2013.

**LANA:** Nuclear engineer from Damascus. Interviewed by Skype from Nordenham, Germany, on December 5, 2016.

**MAHER**: Schoolteacher from al-Latamneh village in the Hama Governorate. Interviewed in Berlin, Germany, on July 19, 2016.

**MAHMOUD**: Actor from Homs city. Interviewed in Amman, Jordan, on September 20, 2012.

**MARCELL**: Activist and blogger from Aleppo city. Interviewed in Gaziantep, Turkey, on January 11, 2016.

**MESUD**: Activist from Qamishli in the Hasakah Governorate. Interviewed in Gaziantep, Turkey, on October 1, 2013.

**MIRIAM**: Young woman from Aleppo city. Interviewed in Amman, Jordan, on September 20, 2012.

**MOHAMMED**: Professor from Jawbar in the Damascus suburbs. Interviewed in Abu Dhabi, United Arab Emirates, on March 16, 2016.

**MUNTASER**: Journalist from Daraa city. Interviewed in Irbid, Jordan, on August 25, 2013.

**MUSA**: Professor from Aleppo city. Interviewed in Berlin, Germany, on July 11, 2016.

**MUSTAFA**: Barber from Salamiyah in the Hama Governorate. Interviewed in Istanbul, Turkey, on March 24, 2016.

**NABIL**: Musician from Damascus. Interviewed in Berlin, Germany, on August 29, 2016.

**NADIR**: Activist from Ras al-Ayn in the Hasakah Governorate. Interviewed in Gaziantep, Turkey, on October 5, 2013.

**NUR**: Beautician from Aleppo city. Interviewed in Berlin, Germany, on August 13, 2016.

**OMAR**: Playwright from Damascus. Interviewed in Beirut, Lebanon, on January 12, 2016.

**OSAMA**: High school student from al-Qusayr in the Homs Governorate. Interviewed in Copenhagen, Denmark, on June 23, 2016.

**RAMI**: University graduate from the Yarmouk Palestinian refugee camp. Interviewed in Lund, Sweden, on June 18, 2016.

**RANA**: Mother from Aleppo. Interviewed in Antakya, Turkey, on September 9, 2013.

**RIMA:** Writer and activist from Suwayda city. Interviewed in Amman, Jordan, on October 7, 2012.

**SADIK:** Veterinary assistant from village in the Suwayda Governorate. Interviewed in Berlin, Germany, on July 24, 2016.

**SAFA:** Mother from Homs city. Interviewed in Tripoli, Lebanon, on January 28, 2016.

**SALAH:** Landscape designer from Naima village in the Daraa Governorate. Interviewed in Irbid, Jordan, on October 13, 2012.

**SAMI:** University graduate from Damascus. Interviewed in Beirut, Lebanon, on January 31, 2016.

**SANA:** Graphic designer from Damascus. Interviewed in Beirut, Lebanon, on January 30, 2016.

**SHADI:** Accountant from the Hama Governorate. Interviewed in Reyhanlı, Turkey, on September 26, 2013.

**SHAFIQ:** Business school graduate from Daraya in the Damascus suburbs. Interviewed in Gaziantep, Turkey, on October 4–6, 2013.

**SHAM:** Relief worker from Douma in the Damascus suburbs. Interviewed in Stockholm, Sweden, on June 26, 2016.

**TALIA:** Television news correspondent from Aleppo city. Interviewed in Gaziantep, Turkey, on January 12, 2016.

**TAREK:** Doctor from Ghouta in the Damascus suburbs. Interviewed in Antakya, Turkey, on September 22, 2013.

**TAYSEER:** Lawyer from Daraa city. Interviewed in Irbid, Jordan, on August 14, 2013.

**UM KHALED:** Mother from Aleppo city. Interviewed in Tripoli, Lebanon, on January 28, 2016.

**UM NAJI:** Mother from the Yarmouk Palestinian refugee camp. Interviewed in Berlin, Germany, on June 22, 2016.

**WADDAH:** Medical school graduate from the Latakia Governorate. Interviewed in Dubai, United Arab Emirates, on March 19, 2016.

**WAEL**: University graduate from Daraya in the Damascus suburbs. Interviewed in Gaziantep, Turkey, on October 2, 2013, and in Halmstad, Sweden, on June 19, 2016.

**WALID**: Poet from the Damascus suburbs. Interviewed in Istanbul, Turkey, on August 28, 2013.

**YASMINE**: Early childhood education expert from the Yarmouk Palestinian refugee camp. Interviewed in Malmö, Sweden, on June 22, 2016.

**YASSER**: Former university student from Aleppo city. Interviewed in Amman, Jordan, on September 20, 2012.

**YOUSEF**: Former medical student from al-Shadadi village in the Hasakah Governorate. Interviewed in Stockholm, Sweden, on July 25, 2016.

**YUSRA**: Mother from Aleppo city. Interviewed in Berlin, Germany, on July 24, 2016.

**ZIYAD**: Doctor from Homs city. Interviewed in Marj al-Hamam, Jordan, on October 2, 2012.

# Introduction

One evening in the fall of 2012, I met Rima on a breeze-filled balcony in Amman, Jordan. Rima was a television screenwriter in Syria before 2011, when she became active in the movement against the authoritarian regime of Bashar al-Assad and then a spokesperson for the network of local committees coordinating protest throughout the country. She was arrested for a few days and went back to work, but regime intelligence agents followed her with threats of ever more frightening punishment. She fled to Jordan, where a friend introduced us. Rima spoke with a delicate voice that belied the boldness of the risks she had undertaken, but not the heavy grief she shouldered for fallen friends and a homeland whose bleeding would not end. Her commitment to what she cherished as a revolution was unshaken. "Syrians defeated the regime the moment they went into the streets," she told me. "We will not allow anyone to steal our dreams again."

In the nearly five years that have passed since that conversation overlooking the hills of the Jordanian capital, I have come to know hundreds of Syrian men, women, and children. They have included housewives and rebel fighters, hair-gelled teenagers and businessmen in well-pressed shirts, die-hard activists and ordinary families caught in the crossfire. Most opposed Assad rule, as do the majority of Syrian refugees as of this writing. While the drivers of forced migration have evolved over time, the majority of those who fled during the first years of the conflict were escaping aerial bombardment and other mortal punishments levied by the regime against individuals and areas challenging its rule.

This book focuses on that slice of the Syrian population. The people with whom I spoke do not represent all of Syria's complex religious-political landscape, and in particular those who support Assad. Nevertheless, they are a population that meets with too few opportunities to represent itself. Politicians and commentators throughout the world talk about Syrians as victims to be pitied, bodies to be sheltered, radicals to be denounced, or threats to be feared and blocked. In the whirlwind of words spoken about Syrians as a global problem, it can be difficult to find chances to listen to actual Syrians, as human beings.

This book offers such a chance. My drive to record Syrians' voices took shape as I watched the 2011 Arab Spring unfold on my computer screen at Northwestern University, where I am a professor of political science specializing in the Middle East. Having dedicated more than twenty years to researching and living throughout the region, I was captivated by the joyous street protests, defiant chants, and inspiring shows of solidarity that shook country after country. Like other observers, I doubted that the revolutionary wave would reach Syria. Compared to other Arab authoritarian regimes that saw mass demonstrations, Syria's single-party police state was more repressive, its military more infused with the regime, and civil society more severely curtailed. Bashar al-Assad's regime enjoyed assets such as a domestically popular foreign policy, the legacy of an extensive welfare state, and generally high regard for a youthful president. Whereas countries such as Tunisia and Egypt were largely homogeneous societies that saw most of their members alienated from the government, Syria was a diverse mosaic in which many citizens from religious minority backgrounds supported the president, who himself comes from the minority Alawite sect. Nevertheless, Syrians went out on the streets. Defying threat of injury, imprisonment, or death, dozens and then hundreds and soon hundreds of thousands of Syrians dared to protest. Or as Rima explained it to me, they dared to dream.

The more closely I followed these protests, the more I craved to discover what they meant to those who risked their lives to participate in them. I wanted to understand how the budding uprising was changing them, and how they were in turn changing the course of history. Given the perilous conditions inside Syria, I searched for stories among the millions who had fled the country. In summer 2012, I traveled to Jordan, where I spent six weeks interviewing any displaced Syrian I could. In 2013, I returned to Jordan and also spent two months in Turkey, where I conducted interviews with a more diverse mix of Syrians from different backgrounds and hometowns. In 2015 and 2016, I returned to spend several more months in Turkey, two weeks in Lebanon, and three months between Germany, Sweden, and Denmark. I continued to interview Syrians wherever I found them: families newly resettled within biking distance of my home in Chicago, decades-old residents of Dubai whom I met on the sidelines of an academic visit, and so on. Each interview connected me to ever-wider circles of Syrians with an ever-broader range of experiences, and brought my chronicling of the conflict into the present.

Along the way, I immersed myself in refugee communities. I roomed with families for weeks, talked in cafés late into the night, and sat at the side of the injured in hospitals and rehabilitation centers. I visited dusty refugee camps, squalid informal settlements, gymnasiums turned shelters, and countless sparse apartments. I did volunteer work that ranged from teaching journalism to eighth graders on the Turkish-Syrian border to distributing clothing in central Berlin. In these and countless other spaces, I played with children, washed dishes, scrolled through photos and videos, inhaled secondhand smoke, and joined meals as exquisite as they were tightly budgeted. And whenever possible, I asked people if I could interview them about their personal stories.

The interviews that I conducted were open-ended chances for individuals to describe and reflect on life before, during, and since the start of the 2011 Syrian rebellion. Interviews ranged from twenty-minute chats to extended group discussions, to personal histories recorded over days—and sometimes continued years later on a different continent. I conducted the majority of interviews in Arabic, a language to which I have dedicated half my life to attaining fluency. This enabled an interviewer-interviewee connection that would have been impossible had I relied on an interpreter. Indeed, it became the basis of lasting friendships, as I remain in contact with many of the individuals whose voices appear in this book.

Getting interviews on paper entailed a two-fold process of transcribing audio-recorded speech and, in most cases, translating speech from Arabic to English. To tackle these time-consuming tasks within a reasonable time frame, I hired, trained, and supervised more than twenty assistants to help. I then spent several months scrutinizing transcripts. Doing so, I was struck, as I had been when carrying out the interviews, by the extent to which personal narratives coalesced into a collective narrative. Palpable overlaps revealed how many individual lives passed through the same stages and grappled with similar issues. Even where interviewees disagreed, they revealed how their personal journeys mapped onto Syria's historical trajectory from authoritarianism to revolution, war, and exile.

I made this trajectory the arc of the book, and culled excerpts from testimonials that I believed could best walk readers through its steps. I chose to reserve the text completely for Syrians' own words; I was convinced that they provided not only personal anecdotes, but also analytical insight that could explain developments in their country without need for my additional narration. This does not mean, however, that the book is without narrative. The narrative lies in the sequencing of entries such that each builds on that which precedes it, connects to those that follow, and divulges a new layer of this multi-layered history. In selecting specific passages to move that narrative forward, I was guided by the twin criteria of representativeness and expressive power. On the one hand, I selected stories that described critical events and central issues that I heard repeatedly and also knew to resonate with the larger universe of already-published audio, visual, and written materials. This gave me confidence that the testimonials that I included spoke to the concerns and experiences of a much broader slice of the Syrian population, and especially those critical of Assad rule. On the other hand, I chose testimonies that conveyed shared themes with especially vivid, intimate human detail. I was drawn to those impactful moments of speech that conveyed not only what happened and how it happened, but also reminded us that it was real human beings who lived it.

I approached the work of excerpting and curating interviews as if making a mosaic. Each testimonial was akin to a precious stone; my mission was to cut from it a piece that displayed its unique gem-like properties and then arrange those gems in such a way that they together constituted a picture greater than the sum of its parts. Cutting was a delicate process. Full interview transcripts could run dozens of pages and bore the free flow of a conversation. People sometimes began with a comment on current events, subsequently jumped to a distant memory, returned to a more recent anecdote, and then circled back to add a detail invaluable for understanding an experience already discussed. In editing such testimonies for length and readability, my challenge was to capture speakers' voices in the literal sense of using their own words and in the figurative sense of relaying the distinct selves communicated by those words. Sometimes pages were needed to capture that voice. Other times, the power of a lifetime was embodied in a few words. The different lengths of entries in the book showcase this rich variety.

I used pseudonyms for all speakers unless I received permission to identify them by name. The alphabetized list before this introduction identifies all speakers with a reference to their profession, hometown, and where and when I interviewed them. An abbreviated reference to the speaker's profession and hometown is also included with each testimonial. I sought to craft passages such that their speakers could say, as one woman did upon reading her entries, "I hear my spirit coming through." My goal for the volume as a whole was to produce a chronicle that Syrians might find, as did another Syrian reader: "There's nothing here that surprises me." For me, this was the highest praise: it meant that, for at least one cross-section of Syrians, I got the story right.

The book is organized in eight parts that reflect the major phases of the Syrian revolutionary experience. The remainder of this introduction complements the personal stories with background on the context within which they unfolded. Some may wish to read this historical overview before diving into the personal voices. Those least familiar with the Syrian conflict might instead prefer to move part by part by reading the voices and accompanying section of the introduction in tandem. Any combination can achieve the goal of this work: to explain the Syrian uprising, war, and refugee crisis, and lay bare, in human terms, what is at stake.

\*   \*   \*

Part I of this book explores Hafez al-Assad's authoritarian rule of Syria from 1970 to 2000. The history of Syria, of course, stretches millennia before that. Seat of some of the oldest continuously inhabited cities in the world, the eastern Mediterranean, also called the Levant, came under Ottoman rule in the early sixteenth century. With the Ottoman Empire's defeat in World War I, the League of Nations carved these Arab areas into separate nation-states under British or French colonial control. France acquired a Mandate in Syria and divided the territory along sectarian lines. Two separate states of Damascus and Aleppo contained Sunni Arab majorities and smaller Christian, Jewish, Shiite, and Ismaili religious communities, as well as distinct Turkmen, Armenian, Circassian, and Kurdish

ethnic communities. The coastal Latakia region was designated a state for Alawites, adherents of a branch of Shiite
Islam who historically had been persecuted. The south-
eastern corner of Syria became a state for the heterodox
ethnoreligious Druze religious minority. Following years
of anticolonial activity enlisting all communities to varying
degrees, France conceded to integrate the different regions
into a single republic. In 1946, Syria became a sovereign
state.

Syria preserved its preindependence parliamentary system dominated by a conservative, traditional elite. Already
weak and unrepresentative, this system was further dis-
credited by Syria's defeat in the 1948 Arab-Israeli War. In
the decades that followed, industrialization, mechaniza-
tion of agriculture, expanding access to education, and
other socioeconomic developments swelled a new middle
class and politicized the peasantry. Youth from rural and
religious minority backgrounds, finding traditional economic and political structures unable to accommodate
their growing aspirations, increasingly joined radical political parties. The Baath Party, a revolutionary movement
committed to Arab unity and socialism, attracted particular support. It also gained a foothold within the army,
where many young men from marginalized communities
had long sought an avenue of mobility.

Against this backdrop of class conflict and ideological ferment, military interventions in politics overthrew seven governments between 1949 and 1963. In that year, army officers affiliated with the Baath Party seized control of the state. The new regime nationalized industries and businesses, redistributed land, and extended welfare services such as education, health care, irrigation, and subsidies. While these reforms mobilized a mass base of support, they provoked opposition from wealthier sectors and rival political movements. Apart from those challenges, the Baath were racked by their own internal divisions, which only worsened after defeat in the 1967 War resulted in Israel's occupation of Syria's Golan Heights.

One of the Baath leaders jostling for power was General Hafez al-Assad, minister of defense and commander of the air force. In November 1970, he sidelined competitors and took power via a bloodless coup.

President Assad replaced decades of political instability with a single party security state. A foreboding military-police establishment, including multiple security services and internal intelligence agencies, monitored, vetted, and punished both citizens and other state personnel. Assad staffed security forces with personal loyalists and disproportionately reserved leadership posts for trusted members of his own Alawite community. The Baath Party, operating through thousands of cells and branch offices throughout the country, similarly acted as an instrument of local surveillance and control. It also co-opted millions with the professional and economic privileges of membership.

Beyond formal institutions, Assad used alliances across society to remind citizens of the benefits of remaining in the regime's good graces—and the costs of opposing it. While promoting an image of stalwart protection of religious minorities, he reached out to win the allegiance of powerful actors within the Sunni Muslim majority, including clergy. He appeased the traditionally Sunni business class by allowing them to continue and gradually expand private enterprise and trade. At the same time, he sustained a populist welfare state, including dramatically inflated employment in an enormous public sector. Such patronage politics sustained support from key constituencies such as peasants and workers. Yet it also saddled the state with an unsustainable burden of waste, debt, and corruption. Ultimately the economy failed to deliver the growth required by a burgeoning population.

Where real backing for the regime was not forthcoming, coerced obedience filled the gaps. Farcical elections produced 99 percent mandates to renew the president's tenure, while ubiquitous statues and pictures brought his gaze into public spaces. Schools and state-controlled media taught people what they could and could not say, while compulsory military service gave young men a further dosage of disciplining. Networks of covert informants policed society and encouraged it to police itself. Sensing that nowhere was safe, parents reared children on the saying "Whisper, the walls have ears." A pervading threat of punishment was not simply imagined. An Emergency Law instituted in 1963 gave security forces sweeping powers to censor expression, restrict citizens' assembly, seize properties, and arrest, interrogate, and detain anyone at will. Political prisoners were not only denied due process, but also subjected to overcrowding, filth, hunger, disease, and multiple forms of torture.

These interlocking structures and practices were sufficient to preempt most organized opposition. The exception that proved the rule came in the late 1970s, when Assad's controversial military intervention in the Lebanese civil war ignited Syrians' already-accumulating grievances with inflation, corruption, and security force abuses. Many civic and professional associations agitated for human rights. The Muslim Brotherhood, a branch of the Islamist political movement founded in Egypt in the 1920s and a powerful opponent of Baath rule in Syria, began a violent campaign against regime targets. Authorities responded by indiscriminately killing, imprisoning, or disappearing tens of thousands of citizens. When Muslim Brotherhood militants led an insurrection in the city of Hama in 1982, Assad launched a brutal assault that flattened whole neighborhoods and left tens of thousands of civilians dead. This trauma, which Syrians referred to euphemistically as "the events," warned generations of how the state would respond to challengers.

*   *   *

Part II probes Bashar al-Assad's first decade in power, from 2000 to 2010. Hafez al-Assad had groomed his eldest son, Basel, to be his successor. Basel's death in a car accident in 1994 transferred that expectation to the president's second son, Bashar, then an ophthalmology student in London. When Hafez died in 2000, Bashar fell six years shy of the Syrian constitution's requirement that the president be at least forty years old. The Syrian parliament immediately amended that clause. Nominated by the Baath Party as the only candidate, Bashar was elected president in a national referendum by a reported 99.7 percent of voters.

Many Syrians welcomed their new head of state, who presented himself as a youthful and modern reformer. In an unprecedented political opening that became known as the "Damascus Spring," civil society spearheaded new forums for debate and petitions demanded greater freedoms and rule of law. Old walls of fear appeared to be crumbling until the government, not ready for change after all, launched a crackdown. Arrests and trials of activists, organizational closures, and malicious rhetoric throttled the movement, at least temporarily.

Meanwhile, neoliberal economic reform opened the country to new consumer goods and commercial possibilities. Many in the urban middle and wealthy classes rejoiced in access to novel comforts. Unleashed without political accountability or oversight from an independent judiciary, however, privatization and trade liberalization allowed corruption to reach unprecedented heights. A new class of crony capitalists, at their fore Assad's extended family, because conspicuously rich. As power and wealth became concentrated in a narrower elite, the regime increasingly abandoned its traditional working-class base. Inflation, unemployment, crumbling infrastructure, and cutbacks in state subsidies and services precipitated rising rates of poverty and inequality. Neglect of the countryside aggravated rural destitution, particularly after drought—and the government's mismanagement of it—swept areas of the northeast and south from 2006 to 2010.

The sense of economic despair and choked aspirations were especially acute among the more than half of the population under the age of twenty-four. A good portion were university graduates who could not break through layers of favoritism and nepotism to find work. Simmering discontent broke into the streets in 2004, when antagonistic chants at a soccer match in the predominantly Kurdish city of Qamishli transformed into a Kurdish uprising. Mass demonstrations became riotous until the army's deployment of tanks, helicopters, and thousands of troops killed dozens and brought the unrest to an end.

After a decade in power, Bashar al-Assad remained personally popular. Yet many Syrians saw their lives worsen under his rule. Few who longed for greater civil liberties, rule of law, government accountability, and fair economic opportunity dared to voice demands publicly. For most people most of the time, to dream of freedom seemed foolish, and to fight for it, reckless.

\*       \*       \*

Part III details the launch of the Syrian revolution. Its roots lay in the yearning for change that fueled mass demonstrations across the authoritarian Middle East. In December 2010, when a self-immolation sparked demonstrations in rural Tunisia and security forces responded with repression. Outraged citizens spread protest throughout the country, forcing the much-loathed President Zine el-Abidine Ben Ali to flee in mid-January 2011. Egyptians then took to the streets and, defying police violence during eighteen days of far-reaching mobilization, pushed the long-ruling Hosni Mubarak to resign as well.

As what became known as the Arab Spring extended to Yemen, Bahrain, Libya, and beyond, many observers believed that Syria—a "kingdom of silence"—would be immune from the regional tide. Nevertheless, many ordinary Syrians were elated by these previously unimaginable shows of people's power, and some began to express political dissent in new ways. Against this backdrop, a spontaneous protest in the Hareeqa market of old Damascus showed surprising boldness, as did vigils outside the Egyptian and Libyan embassies in solidarity with revolts in those countries. Syrian expatriates issued online calls for nationwide protest on March 15. Damascus and other localities witnessed small demonstrations, but armed personnel quickly suppressed them.

Meanwhile, in the city of Daraa on the Jordanian border, security forces arrested children after antiregime graffiti appeared on a school wall. When relatives beseeched local officials for their release, the notorious provincial police chief dismissed them with a vulgar insult that incensed the entire community. A march the next day swelled into a mass demonstration during which security forces killed two unarmed protestors. Subsequent funerals launched larger demonstrations, and subsequent demonstrations resulted in still more funerals. Protestors recorded events with mobile phones, producing videos that made their way online, to satellite news channels, and the knowledge of citizens elsewhere in Syria and the world.

One week after the start of protest in Daraa, tens of thousands joined in demonstrations across the country. The regime's response—offering some measures of appeasement while suppressing gatherings with force—sparked further indignation and resolve. A widespread expression captured what this historic moment meant for those who discovered themselves and their nation in its unfolding: Syrians broke the barrier of fear.

\*    \*    \*

Part IV takes a closer look at the regime's efforts to repress the protest movement and protestors' efforts to sustain the movement, nonetheless. Twelve days and sixty-one deaths passed before Assad delivered his first televised address. Many Syrians insist that had he offered remorse for the bloodshed, as well as indications of meaningful change, they would have cheered his leadership. Instead, by denouncing unarmed protestors as terrorists and traitors to be crushed, he brought more people out into the streets.

The uprising swelled, and initial calls for reform escalated into demands for the regime's overthrow.

The United States, European Union, and Arab League imposed sanctions on the Syrian government and eventually called for Assad's resignation. Under pressure, the Syrian government opened a national dialogue with handpicked reform-oriented figures, held parliamentary elections, and repealed the hated Emergency Law. At the same time, with a new Anti-Terrorism Law as cover, the regime arrested tens of thousands on pretexts ranging from participation in protests to being from a town known for protests to no pretext at all. It carried out wholesale torture of detainees, aimed in part at terrifying communities when emaciated neighbors or mutilated corpses returned home. Some bloody acts, such as the massacre of a peaceful vigil in Homs's Clock Square or the brutal torture of a boy in Daraa, became symbols of the regime's apparent readiness to carry out the threat that its loyalists were scribbling on walls at the time. Citizens could choose: either "Assad or we burn down the country."

Taking repression house to house, security forces conducted hair-raising raids of civilian homes. These could entail pounding down doors in the middle of the night, committing murder and rape, and looting or destroying at will. Some raids, like beatings and shootings of protestors on the streets, were carried out by thuggish civilian loyalists whom the population referred to as *shabeeha* (singular: *shabeeh*). When these measures failed, the regime sent tanks and troops into restive communities. Using snipers to enforce curfews, the army cut access to food and utilities, and carried out theft, arson, and summary executions. Independent human rights investigations judged regime actions to constitute crimes against humanity.

Syrians opposed to Assad organized to keep the revolution going. Citizen journalists took up cameras and documented both demonstrations and regime abuses. Activists came together in informal groups dubbed *tanseeqiyat*, or coordination committees. Operating underground to evade arrest, hundreds of committees across the country planned protests, organized relief for besieged communities, provided medical care for the wounded, and attended to myriads of other challenges as they emerged. In bringing together citizens of different walks of life, these grassroots efforts embodied the revolution's ambition to break from the hierarchy, atomization, and distrust fostered by the authoritarian state and replace it with a democratic society based on civic engagement, participation, and social solidarity.

The core of the conflict in Syria was a struggle between those who opposed the Assad regime and those who wanted to preserve it or feared that alternatives would be even worse. But this political division overlapped with other economic and social cleavages. Urban and rural working-class folk formed the rebellion's core base of support. Some among the more affluent, especially in the two largest cities, Damascus and Aleppo, were more ambivalent. While Syrians of all religions and ethnicities could be found on different sides of the conflict, polarization took an increasingly sectarian hue. The country's Sunni Muslim majority tended to view the revolt as a struggle that would both bring freedom and rectify disadvantages they faced due to favoritism and abuses of power. Many members of minority communities feared that the rebellion threatened their very existence. Regime propaganda and media actively cultivated such fears, including the charge that the rebellion was fueled by conservative Arab Gulf states' plotting to replace Syria's secular, multicultural character with an Islamic state.

Bloodshed compounded the sectarianizing effects of rhetoric. The fact that the security leadership and majority of civilian shabeeha were Alawite increased Sunni citizens' sense that the sect as a whole was complicit in their oppression. This in turn intensified ordinary Alawites' fears of vengeance. Many became convinced that their collective survival depended on Assad rule, regardless of their own criticism of its wrongdoing or lack of personal share in its spoils. With time, atrocities with sectarian overtones would be committed and suffered by all sides.

\*    \*    \*

Part V examines the militarization of the rebellion. From March to September 2011, the protest movement buried some two thousand dead, yet remained overwhelmingly nonviolent. Eventually, citizens and army defectors took up arms. First, they focused defensively on protecting demonstrators and communities; then, under the banner of the Free Syrian Army (FSA), they carried out attacks on military targets. Lacking preexisting networks and infrastructure, however, the FSA was not an organized force so much as a banner championed by hundreds of autonomous battalions. A Supreme Military Council set up headquarters in Turkey but proved unable to wield command and control. Opposition political bodies formed in exile, first the Syrian National Council and later the National Coalition of Syrian Revolutionary and Opposition Forces, fell similarly short in establishing leadership of the larger freedom struggle.

Gradually, rebels pushed regime forces from territory across the country. The regime pounded those areas with artillery, missiles, airpower, and scorched-earth assaults. When rebels wrestled control of most of Homs, Syria's third-largest city, the regime responded with indiscriminate bombardment that caused rampant destruction. Fighters and a few thousand civilians were eventually besieged in the old city, where many remained without food or medicine for two years before consenting to be evacuated.

Other rebel formations emerged, many oriented toward an Islamist ideology. The al-Qaeda-affiliated Nusra Front announced its birth in January 2012. It traced some of its roots to the mid-2000s, when Assad facilitated the flow of Islamist fighters into Iraq to fight American troops and then, recognizing their hostility to his own regime, imprisoned them upon their return through Syria. When the Syrian uprising was still predominantly peaceful, presidential amnesties released many of these fighters, cunningly infusing the rebellion with terrorists in order to legitimate the regime's claim to be combating terrorism. In April 2013, other al-Qaeda affiliates announced their formation of an even more radical group: the Islamic State in Syria and Iraq (ISIS). Both Nusra and ISIS enjoyed funding, discipline, and swarms of foreign fighters that expanded their presence on the ground relative to that of the FSA.

A series of international monitors, cease-fire plans, and peace processes attempted to end the bloody conflict, without effect. Western governments condemned Assad, yet did not offer the antiaircraft weapons or no-fly zone demanded by the opposition to protect civilians from his assaults. The United States, Saudi Arabia, Qatar, Turkey, and other private and state sources funneled funding to the rebels, but it came through disparate channels to different contacts, and promoted competing interests. Skeptics of the Syrian revolt criticized its fragmentation and disorganization, and highlighted its divisions as reason to hesitate giving greater assistance. Rebels insisted that chaos in the external sources and distribution of resources was the gravest cause of disunity, if not also corruption, among their ranks.

The Assad regime enjoyed more decisive external support. Iran, Russia, Iraq, and the Lebanese Hezbollah movement provided the Syrian regime with money, weapons, fighters, and ultimately airstrikes against its foes. This support was not only vital in reinforcing the regime, but also dramatically illustrated how the Syrian war was embroiling the region at large.

*　*　*

Part VI probes the experiences of civilians living this brutal multidimensional war. By the summer of 2013, rebels pushed government forces from some 60 percent of the country, gaining control over large swaths of its north and west. A dramatic battle transpired when rebels launched an offensive to take Syria's largest city and economic capital, Aleppo. The operation stalemated in the division between the city's western neighborhoods, which remained with the regime, and its poorer eastern areas, which came under rebel control.

In these and other territories that the opposition regarded as liberated, civilians and fighters established local councils to govern and provide services to the population. In Aleppo, residents elected their local representatives. There and elsewhere, populations struggled to cope with electricity, water, and food shortages, vast physical destruction, devastated economies, rebel rivalries, and ongoing shelling and bombing by the Assad regime and its allies—the only forces that controlled the skies. Whether creating playgrounds out of recycled missiles, forming rescue teams to salvage strangers from under rubble, or renewing demonstrations whenever cease-fires offered fleeting respite, such communities mustered the resilience to keep going. Residents of government-held neighborhoods likewise steeled themselves and buried their dead, many killed by mortars fired indiscriminately by rebels in adjacent areas.

In a war whose greatest victims were civilians, terror took many forms. Imposing shockingly brutal rule in the areas that it seized, ISIS raped women and girls, enlisted child soldiers, and committed murder through such grue-some means as public beheadings. Far greater numbers of casualties occurred at the hands of the Assad regime. The single greatest killer was barrel bombs, typically oil drums or gas tanks packed with explosives and shrapnel and dropped on areas that included schools, hospitals, markets, and residential neighborhoods. Government forces also imposed strategies of surrender-or-starve by encircling communities and preventing entry of food. An iconic pho-tograph from the Yarmouk Palestinian refugee camp near Damascus offered a glimpse of what happened on the rare occasions that the United Nations, operating in Syria only at the whims of its government, was permitted to reach be-sieged areas: ghosts of men, women, and children queued to receive food packages, as far as the eye could see.

August 2013 registered a new level of war crimes when chemical weapons, carried by rockets that experts insist only could have been fired by the Syrian army, hit the Damascus suburb of Ghouta and killed some fourteen hundred individuals, more than four hundred of them children. U.S. declarations that use of chemical weapons was a red line raised many Syrians' hopes for decisive intervention. Yet threats of a strike came and went, and when the United States finally did dispatch planes in the summer of 2014, it was with the mission of targeting

ISIS, not Assad. By March 2015, the United Nations reported that 6 percent of Syria's population had been killed or injured, some 80 percent lived in poverty, and the majority of children no longer attended school. Satellite images showed a country literally "plunged into darkness," with 83 percent of lights gone out.

\* \* \*

Part VII follows Syrians who fled their country in search of refuge near and far. As of early 2017, more than half of Syria's prewar population of 22 million had been forced from their homes since 2011. Estimates suggest that 7 million were internal refugees, 4.9 million were refugees in countries neighboring Syria, and about one million were seeking asylum in Europe.

Many refugees were displaced within Syria several times before leaving its borders. The decision to flee was usually a painful one. People abandoned homes in which they had invested their life savings and neighborhoods that were the repository of their life memories. They often left some extended or nuclear family behind.

Refugees' first stop outside Syria was usually one of the countries on its borders. Without opportunities for asylum or permanent residence, most Syrians there lived in a kind of precarious limbo. An estimated half of the 1.5 million

Syrian children were not in school. Only a small fraction of refugees obtained legal permission to work, and those who were lucky enough to find jobs in the informal sector usually endured conditions and wages that locals would not tolerate. Others, including mothers and children, were reduced to begging or selling trifles on the streets.

Host countries struggled under the burden of the refugee influx just as refugees struggled to build dignified lives. Jordan's Zaatari camp, haphazardly raised in a desert prone to sandstorms in summer and floods in winter, became the country's fourth-largest city. In Lebanon, Syrian refugees totaled approximately a quarter of the population. In the absence of official refugee camps, hundreds of thousands rented shacks or plots for tents in squalid informal settlements. Turkey led other states in extending what it dubbed "temporary protection" to nearly three million Syrians, as well as relatively robust chances to earn some income. Yet the building blocks of a stable future, such as legal standing and educational opportunities, remained insufficient.

It was one thing to suffer the hardships of life near the border for a year or two while waiting each day for news that it was safe to return home. But as time dragged on, and international aid programs fell further behind need, refugees looked for longer-term alternatives. Syrians could typically apply for asylum upon arriving in Europe or North America; the challenge was getting there. A fortunate few received visas to relocate legally. Others used whatever resources and resourcefulness they could rally to smuggle themselves to what they hoped would be safer quarters. The wealthy could afford exorbitant sums for fake passports and forged visas to get to Europe by airplane. Others exhausted their savings, sold their possessions, or borrowed widely to pay smugglers to get them across the Mediterranean by boat.

At first, the main choice was the long, arduous journey from Egypt or Libya to Italy. Then, in 2015, Macedonia lifted restrictions that enabled refugees to pass from Greece through the Balkans to western and northern Europe. This overland opening encouraged huge numbers of refugees to travel to Greece from Turkey, a sea passage that was shorter, safer, and less expensive. A billion-dollar trafficking industry emerged, maximizing profits by packing throngs of desperate individuals into rickety or inflatable boats. Thousands drowned at sea. Some who instead smuggled themselves overland, like the seventy-one people found asphyxiated in a truck on a road in Austria, also died en route.

The record 1.3 million migrants and refugees who made it to Europe in 2015 were thus, in some senses, the lucky ones. While they came from across the globe, nearly 30 percent were Syrian. Refugees trekked across Europe by foot, bus, car, and rail in journeys that could entail weeks of sleeping on the streets, trudging through the rain, carrying babies, and dodging criminals or arrest. More than a third of asylum seekers went to Germany, encouraged by Chancellor Angela Merkel's decision to open her country's borders and suspend, for Syrians, the Dublin Protocol stipulation that refugees remain in their EU country of entry. Sweden's generous asylum policies made it the second top destination, with arrivals peaking at ten thousand a week.

For many Syrians, the start of a new life in Europe was the third in a succession of traumas. The trauma of war was followed by the trauma of a death-defying journey, only to be eclipsed by the trauma of disappointed expectations upon arriving in the West. While European newspapers filled with fears about integrating newcomers of a different culture or religion, most refugees remained overwhelmed by the legal and economic nuts and bolts of survival. For many, life was defined by waiting: waiting for residency permits and other bewildering bureaucratic paperwork, waiting to move out of refugee shelters that ranged from former insane asylums in isolated forests to the hangars of a defunct airport in Berlin, waiting to learn enough of the new language to start looking for work, waiting to be reunited with family scattered across continents, or waiting for some piece of good news from home.

By 2016, Europe had largely closed its borders, leaving some sixty thousand refugees stranded in Greece pending either asylum elsewhere on the continent or deportation. The poorer, overburdened countries neighboring Syria also severely tightened restrictions, even as tens of thousands of people languished in sometimes starving conditions on the Syrian side of their borders. Such was the state of the worst refugee catastrophe since World War II when, in August 2016, the United States accepted its ten thousandth Syrian refugee.

*   *   *

Part VIII concludes with testimonials that struggle to make sense of these tumultuous events. A different group of speakers, such as those who support the Assad regime or those who remain in Syria, might offer a different set of reflections. The voices here bring to light the human significance of the Syrian rebellion for those who shared its longing for change. Mixing pride, guilt, sorrow, courage, and hope, their pained words challenge us to think about who we might be if faced with the same trials of revolution, war, and exile. One wonders what might have been different had we listened to Syrians' voices earlier. It is not too late to listen now.

# Part I

# AUTHORITARIANISM

Fadi, theater set specialist (Hama)

A Syrian citizen is only a number. Dreaming is not allowed.

## Hosam, computer programmer (al-Tel)

When you meet somebody coming out of Syria for the first time, you start to hear the same sentences. That everything is okay inside Syria, Syria is a great country, the economy is doing great . . . It'll take him like six months, up to one year, to become a normal human being, to say what he thinks, what he feels. Then they might start . . . whispering. They won't speak loudly. That is too scary. After all that time, even outside Syria you feel that someone is listening, someone is recording.

# Mohammed, professor (Jawbar)

There are differences in Syrian society, as in any society. Despite those differences, we recognize each other as Syrians. The key problem has been how to build and how to manage a state.

The Syrian state inherited a Syrian army designed by the French, and the French designed it to divide and rule. They appealed to religious minorities to go into the army. Minorities were in an economic situation where they naturally wanted jobs. The French saw that, and at the same time wanted to put them against the Sunni majority, which opposed the French. The result was an army that drew too heavily on minority communities.

The Baath Party came along with an idea of pan-Arabism. This brought Syrians of different backgrounds together, but did not honestly address the problem that Syria is multicultural and multiethnic.

Hafez al-Assad used the Baath Party. He was a military person and didn't really believe in democracy or pluralist politics or all of those liberal ideas that other national figures believed in at that time. He relied on Alawites more than others, even though he later killed a lot of them because they were his rivals. It was pragmatic to use primordial relationships to consolidate power, but it ultimately created even more divisions in Syria.

Assad was a shrewd politician. He managed various players within the Syrian mosaic and patched together a system loyal to him. He allied himself with the traditional urban merchant class and gave them space to make money. At the same time, he kept the underprivileged communities happy with trickle-down state funds, like subsidies for workers and peasants. He allied with traditional Sunni clerics, because he knew that they had control over the religious narrative in society. In the late 1970s, the Muslim Brotherhood had its own vision and used force to try to bring it into effect. Assad used his alliance with clerics to fight the Brotherhood, and some of those clerics, amazingly, stood by him and then his son. There was opposition to him from the left, and he destroyed that, too.

## Issam, accountant (rural Aleppo)

In my opinion, there used to be coexistence, but under security pressure and judicial control. It wasn't real
coexistence. You couldn't even say to someone, "You're
Kurdish, or you're Sunni or Shiite." It was forbidden;
you'd be fined or punished.

We weren't educated about the different people in the
country, so there wasn't real integration. Arabs didn't
know about Kurdish culture. Arabs and Kurds knew nothing about Turkmens. We'd hear that there were people
called Syriacs and Assyrians, but who are they and how do
they live? We didn't know. The Druze? You know that they
live in Syria, but what is their culture and what do they
want? We were all just groups of strangers. A country of
closed communities, held together by force.

# Abdul Rahman, engineer (Hama)

There was an attempted military coup against Hafez al-Assad, but it failed and the Muslim Brotherhood escaped to Hama, which was the capital of its movement in Syria. The army invaded the city from many directions. They started with shelling, and then chose neighborhoods in which to start killing people. In one neighborhood they gathered males over thirteen years old and executed them. They left the corpses so people could see them.

The army came to my grandparents' neighborhood and took four of my uncles. A few days later, they invaded my parents' neighborhood and started kidnapping men in the same way. My father told my mother that he might never come back. But then my dad's best friend called the commanding officer and told him to halt the executions because all the people they'd detained were government workers. He said, "This is a friendly neighborhood, they all work for us." And it was true: My father was a member of the Baath Party. Two of my uncles who got killed were members of the Baath Party, too.

And that's how my father survived. My alcoholic uncle also survived. When the army came to his house, he was naked and kept shouting, "Viva Assad, viva Hafez, viva the military!"

My grandmother went crazy after they took her sons. She never believed that they were killed. My father kept asking people and kept searching. He even went to the cemetery, where he saw mountains of shoes. He dug and dug in the hope of finding his brothers' shoes, just so he could have some evidence that they were killed. He told me that there was blood all over the place and the smell was so bad that he was fainting. But he kept digging, digging, digging. He dug without success.

## Aziza, school principal (Hama)

I'm from Hama, but wasn't there in 1982. I later returned to work as principal of a school. People used to come and talk with me, and each had a story. You can't imagine how they raped the women, how they stole and looted. A relative told me that she saw bodies tied together and tossed into the Orontes River. A friend was a doctor at the hospital where injured regime soldiers were brought for treatment. One died and when they gathered his things they found piles of gold in his pockets. She told me that she took it to the officer and told him that it should be returned to its rightful owners. He swore at her. "Return the gold to his body. Those are spoils of war."

They played with people's lives like it was a game. People said that the troops used to enter a neighborhood, gather all the men, line them against the wall, and shoot them. Once, there was a delay in the firing orders. The soldiers asked what to do and the officer told them to pull the men's pants down. He said, "If they're wearing short underwear then they're with us, so let them live. If they're wearing long underwear then they're terrorists, so kill them."

It was winter and most of the men were wearing long

underwear, and they killed them. One man was left whose underwear was to the knee. It wasn't too long or too short. The soldiers asked what to do. The officer said, "Leave him. He'll spread the word about what he witnessed here, and that will serve us." And so the man survived.

## Kareem, doctor (Homs)

I was born in 1981, at a time when many people were being arrested or killed. The regime told people that they had
no right to ask about their family members in prison. If
they asked, they risked getting arrested themselves. So I'm
from a generation in which dozens of my friends didn't
know whether their fathers were dead or alive.

We're Muslims and our community is conservative. Just
like Christians pray in church, we pray at home. But people had to pray in secret. My family said that if someone
called for my dad while he was praying, I should say that
he couldn't come to the phone because he was in the bathroom. They told me that if the regime knew that someone
was praying, it would think that he had Islamist tendencies, and there would be consequences to pay. I was just a
child, but I was trained to lie for the safety of my family.

## Iliyas, dentist (rural Hama)

Syria had the appearance of being a stable country. But in my opinion, it wasn't real stability. It was a state of terror. Every citizen in Syria was terrified. The regime and authorities were also terrified. The more responsibility anyone had in the state, the more terrified he was. Nobody trusted anyone else. Brother didn't trust brother. Children didn't trust their fathers. "Don't talk, the walls have ears." If anyone said anything out of the ordinary, others would suspect that he was a government informant just trying to test people's reactions and gather a sense of what was going on.

It is a regime based on command and obedience. If it gives to a citizen, it gives him more than he deserves. And if it punishes a citizen, it punishes him more than he deserves. The more corrupt a person is, the easier it is for the regime to use him as an instrument however it wants. And for that reason the more likely he is to rise through the ranks and obtain a high position.

Every state institution re-created the same kind of power. The president had absolute power in the country. The principal of a school had absolute power in the school. At the same time, the principal is terrified. Of whom? Of the janitors sweeping the floor, because they're all government informants.

# Fouad, surgeon (Aleppo)

I graduated from medical school in 1982. I had very good grades and wanted to pursue PhD-level studies. The only way to do that was to go abroad. But to go, you needed approval from the security forces.

One day I was in the cafeteria with a group of friends. Someone from the intelligence services approached us and said that he wanted to speak with me. The Baath Party had its own office in every department in the university, and he took me there.

He said, "We'll try to be nice. We won't ask you many questions. Just be good with us. If anything happens when you're abroad, let us know." I told him that I didn't want to be an informant. Later I got the news: they rejected my application. One of my dreams was broken.

I spent the next four years doing my residency at a hospital in Aleppo. Then, to do general surgery, I was required to pass three exams. I took the written exam. When I came home I saw terror in my father's face. He said that the Political Security Service had come by and asked for me.

I went to their offices the next morning. They take your ID and then you sit and sit and sit. No one says a word to you. That's the technique they use. After six hours, some-one said that the officer wanted to see me.

I went. He said, "Congratulations, you passed your first exam. When is the next one?"

I said, "Next week."

He said, "I think you'll pass that, too. We're very proud of you. What's your plan for the future?"

I said, "Maybe I'll open a clinic or work in the hos-pital."

He said, "That's fine. We've heard that you're a good person. . . . So we need you to work with us."

I said, "What sort of work?"

He said, "It's not about politics. You're a doctor. Patients come to see you, you might notice something wrong. You can tell us the problems of the people."

I said, "But this isn't my job. You have other people who report to you. You can get this from them."

He said, "We can't get the right information from an informant who isn't educated. You'll have patients, friends, colleagues. You'll be invited to social events . . ."

I said, "But I'm just not that person."

He said, "Why are you being stubborn? Half of your friends write reports for us."

I said, "Okay, so why do you need me?"

And then he said, "You know, I can leave you here for another week."

That's when I realized that I was being threatened. I knew it would be easy for them to leave me for ten days or weeks or months . . . I could miss all the exams.

I said, "You prevented me from going abroad to study. Many get permission to leave. They promise that they'll return, but never do. I didn't flee the country. I kept my life in Syria. I am useful for people. If you want to keep me here, I have no power to prevent that. But I won't be useful for you or anyone else."

He paused and then threw my ID back at me, angrily. "Get out," he said. "Just know that it will be difficult for you to find work with the government."

I left. And later I passed my exams.

## Salah, landscaper (rural Daraa)

We don't have a government. We have a mafia. And if you speak out against this, it's off with you to *bayt khaltu* ["your aunt's house"]. That's an expression that means to take someone to prison. It means, forget about this person, he'll be tortured, disappeared. You'll never hear from him again.

# Tayseer, lawyer (Daraa)

I was working as a government employee. At the same time, I was involved in opposition politics and human rights organizations. I was constantly under surveillance. My house, my phone, my contacts—I was always being followed. In 1987, I joined a new political party. And that year I was arrested.

I spent the next eight and a half years in prison. For the first six months, my wife had no idea where I was.

Prisons in Syria are among the most terrifying on the planet. The reason is simple: Human life means nothing to them. I was in a special wing for political prisoners and was harshly tortured from the beginning. We were completely disconnected from the rest of the world.

The day began when they opened the door and we'd go out to a small yard for exercise. Then we'd read and do study sessions. If someone had studied English or French, he'd give lessons. Among the prisoners were many different professions: doctors, lawyers, engineers . . . it was like a university. Soon after lunch, they'd lock us up again, and that was it.

We were about four hundred prisoners spread out over seven rooms. Health conditions and food were terrible. The prison guards used to manipulate us, especially during visits from our families. They'd extort money from our relatives and steal the gifts they brought for us.

One of the most painful things for me was missing my son's childhood. He grew up seeing me only through wire netting during visits. It's hard to see your son and not be able to embrace him. Not be able to ruffle his hair or give him a piece of candy. You can't take him to school or sit him on your lap. When my son was four, he broke his leg and was in a cast. I wasn't allowed to give him a kiss.

These little details mattered a lot.

My brother died while I was in prison. Other relatives died, too, and I wasn't able to see them. My father became ill, and I couldn't take him to the hospital. Holidays, marriages . . . they'd come and go and you weren't there. No cinema, no theater, no personal security. You miss everything that is beautiful and you experience everything that is ugly. In eight years I didn't see a tree.

It was years before my case went before an extralegal security court. The judge passed rulings on thirty people in fifteen minutes. There was no trial, no lawyers. There were no specific charges, except for those that they always had on hand: organizing a secret organization, spreading false information about the regime, attempting to change the regime, publishing and disseminating rumors, or undermining the authority of the government. They sentenced me to five years for some charges; since I'd already served those years, the sentence was dropped. Other prisoners and I were granted a pardon for the remaining charges.

I returned home. My absence had been so absolute. It was like a caveman coming out into the light. I didn't recognize anything anymore. The country had changed. Kids who were little when I left were teenagers when I got back. My own son had become a young man.

My ability to travel was severely restricted. My brothers and sisters were interrogated and also forbidden from traveling. Some people were afraid to have any sort of relationship with me because I remained suspect in the eyes of the regime. For any small thing I wanted to do, I had to get the approval of a security agency. My house was under surveillance, my phone under surveillance. I moved from a small prison to a big one.

## Ghayth, former student (Aleppo)

You're twenty years old and at the peak of your potential, and you have to do two years of compulsory military service. You don't go forward with your life, and in fact are pushed backward. It's a system designed to crush and destroy you.

When my oldest brother did his military service he got a bacterial eye infection. The army hospital didn't know how to treat it, and it worsened to the point that he couldn't see out of one eye. He still doesn't see well until today.

When my other brother was doing his military service they had to do drills where they crawled on the ground in the heat. He got a splinter in his foot and it got infected and swelled to twice its size. Later, an Alawite supervisor found a Quran among his personal things. This was prohibited in the army. The supervisor put him in jail on charges that he was part of the Muslim Brotherhood. My parents only got him out by paying a ton of money.

My parents suffered a lot from all of this. So when it came time for me to do my military service, they immediately sent me out of the country. If you work abroad for five years and then pay a fee of $8,000, you can be exempted from the army. So my parents said, "That's it, you're leaving."

## Hadia, therapist (Damascus)

I went to a private Christian school, but even there you could see the government's power and control. We had Hafez al-Assad's picture on our notebooks. People felt scared to draw on them. Sometimes by the end of the year you'd see a mustache or funny face. But it had to be a really old book, one you didn't show in public.

Under Hafez, headscarves weren't allowed in schools. I had to take mine off when I reached the door. Both private and public schools required military uniforms. As girls, we wore this long shirt and military belt, and special shoes, like in the army. From first to sixth grade, you wore this bandanna around your neck, with a little clip that showed that you belong to the Baath Party. In elementary school you were a member of the "Baath Party Scouts," and in middle and high school you became an actual member of the party.

We had to line up in a certain way, like at military attention. The idea was that we were living under an Emergency Law, and we had to be ready to defend the country at all times. Every single morning we'd repeat, "Our pledge is to stand against imperialism, Zionism, and backwardness, and to crush the criminal apparatus of the collaborationist gang, the Muslim Brotherhood." They made the Muslim

Brotherhood into this very, very scary thing. Even saying the name was scary.

The hardest thing was when they'd tell us that there was a pro-regime march the next day. Sometimes you'd think you should stay home sick, but they'd tell you that if you weren't there, they'd come to your house and get your father. They wouldn't actually say that, but we felt like that was what would happen. That was the atmosphere: They will come for us.

You had to get security approval even to have a wedding. You couldn't do anything without feeling that they're controlling it. You knew that the garbage man or person selling fava beans on the highway until two o'clock in the morning were there because they're intelligence agents.

I remember how there were some books that my dad used to hide. He'd say, "Don't ever tell anyone that we have books by these authors at home." I didn't understand. Every year we'd go to the Damascus book fair, and we'd know that some publishers kept books hidden. The books weren't even necessarily political. There was just a cloud of scariness around us, like they wanted you to feel uncomfortable with what you were doing.

## Sana, graphic designer (Damascus)

Teachers taught us that the Palestinian cause was the most important thing: that we have to forget our rights and all the problems in our country so we can fight Israel. My father always said those two things were not related. We can stand with Palestine and have a good country, too. I'd get very upset because what I heard at home was different from what I heard in school, but I couldn't say anything about it.

There were about four hundred girls in school, so I thought that no one would notice once when I didn't sing along with the national anthem. One teacher did. As punishment, she forced me to crawl on my elbows and knees all over the school grounds. I was bleeding and she called me names, like "vile" and "despicable." I'll never forget that.

The school was very dirty. When I was fifteen, two friends and I formed a cleaning committee. The principal got angry. She sent for my father and asked him who was behind this idea and what kind of books I was reading at home. My father told them that I was just a kid and there was no reason to worry.

Around that time, the school stopped art and music classes. Instead, they gave us three hours that they called an "empty period." I'm convinced that the regime chose that word intentionally. It was an "empty" period, not a "free" period. What they wanted was for us to empty our heads. For them, it was better that we do nothing than do something that would make us think or dream. Their goal was to make sure that people's only interest was eating, drinking, and making sure their kids were safe.

# Ayham, web developer (Damascus)

Basically the brainwashing process starts when you go to school: We love the leader, we love the regime, without them the country will collapse . . . You grow up with that in the back of your head, constantly reminding you that we are living due to the grace of the Assad family.

But even as an innocent child you see that the whole system just reeked. It fed on corruption and grew and grew. If you want to get a passport you have to bribe this guy and that guy, and kiss that guy's ass—excuse my language. It was a vicious circle of corruption. From when you're little, you're taught that this is the only way to survive in this country. As an active member of the ruling party, you're going to get better grades and better chances for better schools or jobs. Everything is handled by how loyal you are to the regime, so you're raised on the principle that you have to show your loyalty.

At the same time, we were injected with this hatred of public enemies, even if we didn't really know what that meant. A lot of people thought that by defending the regime they were protecting the national interest. It was like, "I know the regime is corrupt. I know that my kids will have a shitty future under this system. I know that security forces can break down my door and take me to prison and torture me anytime. But I'm not going to be a slave to imperialists and capitalists!"

It was impossible to form any sort of a social bond outside the circles that the regime allowed. School, sports clubs, cultural houses . . . they controlled every place where people could interact and potentially "conspire" against the regime. You couldn't have a normal conversation without being afraid that the guy you met two weeks ago might write a report on you. The regime had eyes and ears everywhere. It might sound unbelievable, but it just became part of our lives.

So everybody blended into the system and became part of it. Everyone was either scared or corrupted or benefiting in some way. All of this generated a kind of creative chaos. The result was that should things collapse, people were likely to turn against each other.

## Adam, media organizer (Latakia)

As a child, you're afraid all the time. You fear the dark, what's under your bed, whatever. But you're not used to grown-ups being afraid.

I remember the first time I truly understood what fear is. It was 1995 and I was six or seven years old. It was the period when they were promoting Basel al-Assad, Bashar's older brother. The expectation was that he'd take up the mantle after his father. I used to see him on TV doing horseback riding and stuff like that. I thought he was a cool guy.

That day my dad and I were going out to play soccer. He was waiting in the doorway when I heard from one of my friends that Basel al-Assad had been killed in a car accident. I shouted, "Hey, Dad, Basel al-Assad died!"

My dad's face changed color. He grabbed me inside the house and locked the door, without saying a word.

There was no need for any explanation. Somehow the way he behaved conveyed the message to me: This is something that needs to be kept silent. The way he snatched my arm, the way he took me inside, the way he closed the door, the way we weren't going to play soccer anymore.

That is when it clicked for me. It crystallized in my head forever. This family, these people in high authority . . . We can't even utter their names. Even their death is scary. Welcome to Syria.

# Part II

# HOPE DISAPPOINTED

## Abdel-Naser, manager (Douma)

Bashar came to power and he said that he was democratic and different than his father. We politically minded people knew that he was lying, but we didn't want it to be recorded in history that there was an opportunity for change and we didn't take advantage of it. As Jean-Jacques Rousseau said, freedom is something that you take, not that you're given.

This opportunity was the "Damascus Spring." We took those lies that he fed us and we created something called the "Forum." We were an oasis of discussion and debate. We started discussing important issues: education, illiteracy, the relationship between Syria and Lebanon, freedom of political activity . . . We'd meet in private houses and bring in a lecturer and sit and talk. We didn't have formal government approval, but we'd send announcements to the Baath Party and invite them to join us. They'd refuse.

The regime tolerated us for a while, but then got worried. More and more university students were attending, and the regime thought we were poisoning the minds of the young generation. So they banned us. All of a sudden, they called us spies and threw us in prison. Security cars started following my wife and me, and then forces broke into my house at 5:30 in the morning and took me away.

We got out of prison and tried again. A group of intellectual and oppositionists issued the "Damascus Declaration." We emphasized that we were working for peaceful, gradual reform because we didn't want the country to descend into war.

The regime again arrested everyone, though this time I managed to escape and hide. All of this proved that it wasn't a new Assad regime, after all. The torture was the same, the secret police were the same, the government was the same. It was the same regime as under Hafez al-Assad, just with a new face.

## Firas, computer engineer (Aleppo)

I began my political activity at the University of Aleppo in October 2000, three months after Bashar al-Assad came to power. We organized a sit-in against Israel's violence against the Palestinians. Three days before, the Baath Party had a huge sit-in, but we didn't participate. I believed in the same cause, but didn't want to support it the way the regime was supporting it.

About three hundred students participated. We blocked traffic for two hours, and the scene shocked everybody. We wanted to test our ability to mobilize people and also wanted to test the regime's reaction. The next day, Baath Party leaders at the university called us to their office. They understood what we were up to, and their message was very clear: Any political initiative taken in this country can only be done under control of the government and the party.

Our group kept working in secret. In March 2003 we organized an open sit-in against the American war in Iraq. We worked with a great group of people from civil society. There were some Syrian nationalists, communists, Kurdish youth, more than one person from the Islamic movement. We put blankets on the ground, played revolutionary songs, and posted signs. The whole group sat there from morning until dark, and a few would sleep there overnight.

One night around eleven, I left to get food. I didn't get very far before I heard loud noises. Hundreds of people were attacking our demonstration site. They broke everything. After a few days, we realized that the Baath Party had attacked us because we'd organized our sit-in outside its supervision.

In 2004, Bashar al-Assad made a decree to cancel an old rule that guaranteed government jobs for new engineering graduates. We saw this as breaking a contract between students and the government. We spent ten days raising students' awareness about their rights and then prepared a protest.

We were about one thousand students in the demonstration. Members of the security forces and military intelligence and the Baath Party surrounded the protesters. One hundred students were arrested. Eighty-nine were expelled from the university.

We tried to revive our efforts and work with students from the University of Damascus. Three students from our group went there and met with young people active in civil society. But it was clear that the intelligence services were monitoring us, and they arrested everyone. At this point, our initiatives stopped. We realized that circumstances just weren't conducive to the type of work we were doing. We had to find new ways to deal with the regime.

# Mohammed, professor (Jawbar)

I majored in English literature in college. I was friends with the daughter of the minister of finance, and she told me that her dad wanted a translator. Next thing you know, I found myself right in the heart of Assad's government, getting an inside view of how the state was run.

My task was mostly to work with visiting delegations from the International Monetary Fund and World Bank. Sometimes I was even given specific instructions to show them around Damascus and waste their time. It was clear that the state did not want to talk with them seriously.

Once we were in a meeting and the minister got a call from Assad senior. He told us, "The president wants us to hire seventy thousand young university graduates." Assad knew that if all those people were going out on the streets with no jobs, they're going to start protesting. His way of solving this problem was to dump them on the state. You didn't need to know economics to see that this wasn't going to work. The state was already huge—the biggest employer in the country. The problem was just going to get worse and one day it was going to explode.

Assad junior came to power, and the West supported him. But he didn't have the acumen of his father. Senior built the system. He knew every corner of it and he had the skills to bring people together. Junior didn't rise through the system himself. He never fought for it. The guy just studied to be an eye doctor in London and suddenly found himself at the helm of the state.

Assad junior listened to advisers who said, "Let's privatize. You know this socialist thing is finished, the way forward is capitalism." That's great. The only thing is that Syria suddenly came to be owned by two families and their friends. Everybody got a share based on how close they were to the Assad family. Suddenly Syria had new cell phones, but the whole communications network was controlled by Rami Makhlouf, Bashar's cousin.

There was no trickle-down economy anymore. Public welfare went downhill. And then there was a drought, and peasants flooded the cities. The slums around Damascus were massive. The state couldn't manage people's needs.

Once in 2006, I was pulling into a parking lot when this kid suddenly threw himself onto my car. Immediately, all of these police officers appeared. The kid wasn't hurt because the car wasn't moving fast. The police knew it. They told me, "Look, this is the kid's job. We'll help you, but we have to take him to the hospital."

We took him to the hospital and X-rayed him, and it turned out that the kid was full of metal. He had plates here and there—all injuries from previous accidents. The nurses couldn't believe that he'd survived.

The police officers came with me to the hospital and then we all went to the police station. They said, "Look, we need to settle this." And you know how much they wanted? About $100. They divided it among themselves. Even at the police station, everybody was in on the plan and wanted a share. The kid got his share, and I told him, "Why didn't you just ask for the money? You didn't need to throw yourself at the car."

You could see how desperate everyone was. And it was all a result of what Assad senior had done: dumping these people on the state and giving them meager salaries. Do I blame a police officer whose whole salary is $100 a month? When Bashar stopped the trickle-down system, his family became super rich. He and his wife just kept dressing nicely and going out, like cute royalty. He thought, "Everybody loves me and I have no problems." He had no clue.

## Adam, media organizer (Latakia)

Health care was shit. They'd say it's free, but if you wanted real health care you had to pay for it. Universities used to be free. But by the time I went to college, I had to pay for it. And education was crap. I studied economics and business management, but I couldn't actually attend classes because there were too many people. My first year, I went to the lecture hall. It fit like five hundred people. But then I looked at the registration sheet and saw that we were three thousand students in the freshman class. They'd enrolled a lot of people because they wanted their money.

The regime had no willingness to reform the problems in public universities. Instead, their answer was to open new private universities, which charged people thousands of dollars. The gap between rich and the poor just increased, and that added insult to injury.

## Wael, university graduate (Daraya)

If you wanted to get a paper processed or do anything with the state, the employees would humiliate you. If you weren't a member of the Baath Party, they'd treat you like dirt. My dad always told me to join the party because I might not get a job otherwise. I told him that it was hard to get a job regardless.

Once when I was out shopping with my mom, my ID card fell out of my pocket without my noticing it. I went to the police station and the officer said that the political division would contact me.

Later, they called and told me to come to the branch office because the intelligence services were investigating the case of my lost ID. My dad went with me. We entered the room and greeted the officer, who was young enough to be my dad's son. The guy had his feet up on the table. My dad started saying things like, "May God give you thanks! May God protect you, for you are protecting our country!"

The guy asked what I study, and where I work. He asked how many brothers and sisters and aunts I have. He asked whether any of my relatives had traveled outside the country or if I'd traveled outside the country. He knew all of these things, but kept asking anyway. Do you use the Internet? Where do you go online? Do you pray?

Then he asked, "Are you a party member?"

I said, "Yes, I'm an active member." That's a rank above a normal member. My dad started kicking me under the table. He gave me a look as if to say that he couldn't believe that I was lying. I simply thought that if I said I was a party member they might give me a new ID.

The officer continued: "An active member? What division are you in?"

I told him the Damascus suburbs. He asked for my party number. I told him that I forgot it.

"You forgot your party number? When did you last attend a meeting?"

I said about ten months ago. I said that we used to attend every Thursday and talk about Syria's economic accomplishments and stuff like that.

"Who's the leader of your division?" I told him his name was such-and-such, which I knew because some of my friends attended meetings.

He picked up the phone, called someone, and said, "I have a young man here who says he's an active member and I want his party number." The lady on the other line looked me up and couldn't find my name on their lists.

He put his hand over the receiver, lowered it, and told me that I was a liar. I denied it. I knew my friends who were in the party would play along if I asked them. I said,

"I'm an active member! Ask my friends! Everyone in the party knows me!"

He told the person on the phone that I seemed pretty dumb. "He doesn't even know where God has put him on this earth."

I started acting even dumber. "I'm in the party! I went to that one meeting and I got this grade, and we talked about this and that."

The guy started laughing, talking about how stupid I was. I thought, "Whatever happens, I'll just keep lying." In the end, I knew that anything could be fixed with money. My dad would sell the car if necessary.

My dad took out a cigarette and lit it for the officer. He thanked him for his service, saying how we don't lack for anything here in Syria.

Finally the officer told us to leave. After my dad stopped yelling at me, he called a friend who is a Baath member. His friend said, "No problem, I'll add your son to the party lists. I'll register him not just as 'active member,' but at an even higher rank, and going back ten years."

The corruption started from the top and ran throughout.

# Hamoudi, engineering graduate (Aleppo)

I never remember any of my classmates saying that they wanted to be president. Or prime minister, or anything like that. We didn't have big dreams. A kid only dreamt of having a mini-market or something. So what kind of future did that mean we were we going to have? Like hundreds of mini-markets!

This kid raised to want a mini-market sees the kid next to him on track to be a rocket scientist. He is going to feel like nothing and is going to fight him. The regime encouraged that. It didn't just control resources. It also educated people to be against each other.

That's how I felt in college. I have a huge passion for wind energy. For my graduation project, I made a wind turbine. It was just a small one, but it was the first of its kind at the University of Aleppo. It took three months of really hard work and I was proud of it.

My professor told me that I'd definitely get the highest grade. But two other students got the same grade. They didn't do anything significant, but they happened to be friendly with the professors.

It was depressing. There were very smart people who were working hard in Syria. But there was no kind of appreciation. Nobody helped them to achieve.

## Mesud, activist (Qamishli)

In the 1960s, the government adopted its "Arab Belt" policy to alter the demographics of Kurdish areas. It aimed to Arabize the population and change cities' Kurdish names to Arabic names. The Baath regime also passed a law to deny identity cards to Kurdish citizens. My grandfather served in the Syrian army, and the regime even took away his nationality. He and others had no documents saying that they were Syrian, which helped the regime Arabize the area.

Some Kurds got IDs and others did not. It was arbitrary. My brother got an ID card and was considered a citizen. I was one of about four hundred thousand Kurds without IDs. The big problem for us was that we couldn't own anything. My family had to register our house under the name of my uncle, who happened to have an ID. Our family business's warehouse was under the name of another uncle. The car was under someone else's name. Like that. Also we needed the approval of the Political Security Service and State Security Service just to stay in a hotel. When we went to those offices, they spoke to us in such a demeaning way. Because of that, I hated traveling.

# Nadir, activist (Ras al-Ayn)

March 2004 was the Kurdish uprising. I was about fifteen years old when we went out and demonstrated. This was the beginning of a new phase. It created a consciousness within us. We started to organize gatherings and discuss issues. People began to have more courage to speak up about the situation of the Kurds. About a year after the uprising, a group of guys and I made a small, hidden library of books that focused on Kurdish culture. Books on the subject were banned, but we'd get hold of them and trade them among ourselves in secret. We'd hide them under our sweaters and exchange them at night.

# Musa, professor (Aleppo)

People felt wronged by sectarian discrimination in employment. For example, Homs is a mixed city with a Sunni majority, but most of the government employees are from the Alawite sect. In Aleppo there are no Alawites, but you find that it is Alawites who are working for the state. If people were hired on the basis of qualifications, that would be fine. But what does it mean when a qualified person does not get the job, and someone from another sect gets it just because he has connections?

There was a sense of oppression, and this intensified with changes in the economy. People expected more jobs and prosperity. But the shift to the market seemed to enrich some social sectors at the expense of other sectors. High-ranking officers and businessmen close to the regime got rich very quickly through their power, not their skills.

These upstart businessmen undertook ventures that disrupted existing social relations and traditions. In Homs, residents of different sects respected each other. Then new businessmen proposed a development project called "Homs Dream," which aimed at destroying the old city. They tried to intimidate or entice people into selling their property. This had a sectarian dimension because it would dismantle the religious makeup of a traditional part

47

of town. The same thing happened in Aleppo, where old buildings around the citadel were turned into touristic areas. Aleppo is conservative, and some of that real estate had religious significance.

This whole time, poverty was increasing. All of these factors accumulated over Bashar's ten years in power. The poor got poorer and people got angrier, day after day.

## Annas, doctor (Ghouta)

Corruption increased and increased. You'd have to pay a bribe even to leave to go on the pilgrimage to Mecca, which is an Islamic obligation. It reached the point that corruption was in everything—*everything*. There was corruption before, but not to that extent. Everything was getting worse. Things just added up. The glass of water overflowed. There were so many problems that it was ridiculous. Someone had to go out and just say, "No!"

# Part III

# REVOLUTION

# Abu Tha'ir, engineer (Daraa)

The forced resignation of Zine el-Abidine Ben Ali in Tunisia was like a dream. I was one of those Syrians with tears in his eyes. People just couldn't believe it. Impossible! Impossible! My goodness! Was it real? It seemed like a miracle from God . . . we wondered: Could a revolution happen in another country, too?

Tunisia did not have as big a psychological impact as Egypt did. The Egyptian revolution was only eighteen days, but some guys stopped sleeping at night. They followed the news nonstop, all day long: Egypt, Egypt, Egypt.

When it was announced that Hosni Mubarak had resigned . . . wow, I remember that day. People went outside and started to talk. The words began to come out. They'd mention Egypt and say, "Grace be to God." They'd curse Mubarak and say, "He was held accountable. The Egyptian people are achieving a democratic government."

People didn't talk about Bashar. But inside, they wanted their own revolution, too. Outwardly, they just talked about Egypt. Inside they were moved, and had other thoughts.

## Adam, media organizer (Latakia)

So Tunisians had mass demonstrations and Syrians were like, "Hmm, interesting." And then Egypt started. People were like, "Resign already!" And then he resigned. We thought, "Holy shit. We have power."

Then Libya got in line, and this is when Syrians really got interested. Because that guy, Qadhafi, was going to let the army loose on the people straight away. We knew that and Libyans knew that. And Libyans started calling for help, and we thought, "Exactly. This is us." And the international community intervened, saying, "We'll protect the Libyans." And everybody in Syria got the message: If shit hits the fan, people will back us up.

Of course, we would make sacrifices. Some people would die. No doubt about that. But we thought that we'd never have the army attacking us. Because the world would protect us. And we all knew that the minute international forces stepped foot in Syria, the whole army would defect. They would turn on Assad and that would be it.

## Beshr, student (Damascus)

My brother went to the protest outside the Egyptian embassy in Damascus, in solidarity with the Egyptian revolution. When people organized a similar protest outside the Libyan embassy, I decided to go.

By the time I got there, the demonstration was already under way. I saw this girl holding a candle. The wax was melting all over her hand, but she didn't stop her chanting against Qadhafi.

Security guards were surrounding the embassy and recording everyone's faces. I was a little afraid, but also so happy. Later, I called my brother in Saudi Arabia. I told him that I went to the protest and was chanting, "Freedom! Freedom!" I felt like I needed to tell him about it. I said, "You have to experience this." I can't describe it . . . it was like letting all the energy out of you, all the things you'd kept hidden for so many years. You felt like you're not on this earth. Like your soul is just flying somewhere else.

I had an MP3 recorder in my pocket and recorded the protest. That was a dangerous thing to do, so I kept it hidden. I still have the recording. Even now I listen to it every month or so. I just replay it, again and again, and when I listen, I remember exactly how I felt when I held it in my pocket.

## Rima, writer (Suwayda)

For no reason, a police officer assaulted someone in Hareeqa, in the old market in Damascus. In less than five minutes, hundreds gathered and started protesting against the regime. They chanted, "The Syrian people will not be humiliated!" A friend at work told me about it. He was so excited, but I couldn't believe it was real. It was the first time in our lives that we saw or heard about anything of that sort. In less than one hour, videos of the incident were uploaded on YouTube. I watched them and was so happy that I cried. It meant that the revolution in Syria had begun.

## Walid, poet (the Damascus suburbs)

We started talking about the situation in Syria. We agreed that Egypt was ready for an uprising. We figured that we needed at least five more years of political mobilization and activity before we could reach the stage that Egypt had reached. We told each other that we were going to start working toward that goal.

And then there was a call for the revolution to begin on March 15. And we went out. Just like that: The revolution began. Demonstrations were going forward . . . were we going to say, "Wait, we're not ready, we need five more years?" No way—no, no, no, never. A revolution was going forward, we were going to go with it.

# Shafiq, graduate (Daraya)

I was working with computers, so I was on the Internet 24/7. The events in Tunisia and Egypt looked so easy. Our path was open before us. Freedom and dignity were going to come.

The first Facebook page was created: the Syrian Revolution against Bashar al-Assad. They began to write: This happened, that happened, somebody did such-and-such. They set a date: March 15.

I was waiting for March 15 like I was waiting for a rendezvous. It was exciting. I needed to see March 15. The number of people signed up on the Facebook page reached twelve thousand. I imagined that one thousand would show up.

I started meeting with a guy who became one of the first activists in my town. Let me call him Nizar. He told me that I shouldn't go to the demonstration just for the sake of it; I needed to have a specific role. I told him I could do media. He bought me a camera. We bought a shirt and made a hole in the pocket in the shape of a circle. We put the camera through it and I wore a jacket over it. He told me that as soon as I got to the protest, I should turn the camera on and leave it on. When I saw an opportunity to record, I should open my jacket.

We arrived at the Hamidiyah market in Damascus. The first person to start shouting was a man. Word spread that he was from the regime and was encouraging people to protest so they could then arrest us. Then this girl spoke out. Her dad had been arrested in 1982. She shouted, "God, Syria, freedom, and nothing else!"

No one joined her. To be honest, I was scared. Everyone was watching. But Syrians always feel affected by the bravery of a woman. A woman is not braver than me, so I'll join. So I joined in: "God, Syria, freedom, and nothing else!" My voice got louder and louder. The chanting made me forget all about the camera.

Then the security cars came. I withdrew. I felt a sort of fear. I moved back and watched. The security forces arrived with sticks and they started to beat protestors. People from the area joined in and started to hit the protestors, too.

I felt sad. I hated the world and hated life. I felt sadness for the young guys, how they were chanting for the benefit of the entire nation and were beaten. Sadness for why things are the way they are: Why we don't have plans, why we don't have organization, why, why, why? I wanted to drink water, to walk away, to get out of there.

I got in a taxi and told him to take me away. I hadn't filmed anything. I came home upset. Damn, how those guys were beat up. What if it was me who had been beaten up instead? Imagine if I was in their place and everyone was just looking at me, doing nothing.

I sat for hours, and thought, "This is a revolution. This is what happens in a revolution. I could get beat up and I could die. This is for a goal. Either I accomplish the goal or I die." I put pressure on myself: "What's your problem? What happened is normal. This is a corrupt regime; you shouldn't expect anything else from it."

# Ahmed, activist (Daraa)

People say that the revolution started with the call for protest on March 15, 2011. But that wasn't the real beginning. On March 15, people finished demonstrations and went back home. What happened on March 18 in Daraa was completely different.

A security officer named Atef Najib had become head of the Political Security Service in Daraa two years earlier. He is Bashar al-Assad's cousin. This person was a megalomaniac. He asserted his control over everything—borders, customs, other security services, state institutions. Even traffic police. One of his decisions was to forbid people from selling land or real estate without security clearance. Then he gave his own men security clearance and sent them to buy the land at very cheap prices.

So people were already upset. Then the issue of the kids blew things up. One morning, teachers and students arrived at a local school and were surprised to see that someone had written on the wall slogans like "You're next, Bashar" and "It's your turn, doctor."

Until today, no one really knows who wrote it. The school headmaster called the Political Security Service. Agents came but didn't do any sort of investigation. They just needed to arrest somebody so they could write a report to show that they had done their job. They collected kids whose names were written on the wall, even if they'd written them years ago. Most of the kids were younger than sixteen. They tortured the kids and the kids told them everything they wanted to hear. The officers even asked them to give their friends' names, and then the officers went and arrested those friends, too.

The kids' families asked the local head of the Baath Party for his help. When the kids still weren't released, the families formed a delegation to go to talk with Najib. He refused to let the kids go. Instead, he told them, "Forget your children. Go home to your wives and make more children. And if you don't know how, bring your wives and we'll show you how." Word about the insult spread and soon everyone in Daraa knew.

That was Thursday, March 17. Now, let's go back to March 15. People from the leftist parties had planned to protest in front of the Daraa city hall. My father was one of them. When they arrived, they were surprised that the place was filled with security agents waiting for them. So they just walked away, without even raising a banner or chanting a word.

The same night, intelligence agents arrested some of those men, including my dad. They insulted them and told them that they better not even think of demonstrating. The men were set free that night. They decided to have a march the next morning at the mosque after Friday prayers. Why the mosque? Because that's the only place where people can gather without the security services stopping them.

The next day there were security agents stationed at Daraa's two main mosques. So my dad's group went to a new, small mosque, called Hamza wa Abbas. They found no officers there, but they did find the families of the arrested kids.

They had a secret signal to get the protest going. After the imam finished his sermon, someone would shout, "God is great!" Others would repeat after him and they'd all walk toward al-Omari, the major mosque in town. And that's what happened. The kids' families joined the protest, because they were already angry. They reached al-Omari, and people who were praying there joined the protest, too.

We expected that people would sympathize with us, but we were surprised that it took only minutes for everyone to know what was happening when they saw us marching down the street. People joined and started chanting. They came from everywhere: from houses, from streets, from other mosques. And at that moment, we were no longer in control of the situation. It became a public matter.

We hadn't been demonstrating long when we saw helicopters bringing security agents to the municipal stadium. Buses of soldiers were already there. The demonstration gathered at the edge of the valley, which separated us from the part of town where governmental institutions are located. Security forces gathered on the other side.

Police came. The mayor and officer who arrested the kids came, too. They threatened to arrest and kill people if they didn't back down. That made people even angrier. They continued demonstrating and then started to throw stones. The security forces opened fire. Two people were killed. A third was injured and later died from his wounds.

People in Daraa might have gone home that night and tried to find another solution if the regime hadn't shot and killed people. The next day, people went to the funeral for the martyrs and started chanting against the regime. Demonstrations continued and security forces killed more people. And at that point, we realized that protest couldn't be turned back. The situation changed from a political idea to a popular movement.

## Muntaser, journalist (Daraa)

My brother was at the Hamza wa Abbas mosque. Everything was planned in complete secrecy. We didn't know if the protest would actually happen until it did.

I was waiting at al-Omari mosque. When I first saw the demonstration coming toward me, it was a weird feeling. I was so happy that I was going to cry. Nothing like that had ever happened before. Until then, we'd only had pro-regime marches.

The first two martyrs were killed. The second day there was a funeral procession. We didn't expect anyone to participate, because of the killing that had happened the previous day. But we went to the funeral and more than 150,000 people attended. People came from all the surrounding villages.

Everyone agreed that the regime is criminal, but we were afraid to go out. Then the chance came to us. If we lost it, did that mean we'd never be able to go out again? Also, we knew that if we went back, the regime would come and arrest all the young people who had protested that first day. They'd all die in prison. So there was no choice. We entered a road with no return.

# Abu Tha'ir, engineer (Daraa)

The first protest was on Friday. Then there were funerals and more demonstrations. On Tuesday night, a sit-in began at al-Omari mosque. Around three o'clock in the morning, regime forces stormed the mosque from all directions. They killed dozens and injured at lot more. They burnt holy books and wrote things on the wall like "Do not kneel for God. Kneel for Assad."

People in all the surrounding villages heard about the massacre in al-Omari mosque and started coming to Daraa city. They entered, calling, "Peaceful, peaceful, peaceful." And then security forces opened fire on them. Imagine: This village has ten dead. This village has five dead. This village has three dead. This has two dead.

This is how the revolution exploded in the entire province. The government sent dead to every village. The funerals began. And imagine, each funeral becomes a demonstration. If I ever write a book about this, I'll call it *How to Spark a Revolution in One Week*.

## Husayn, playwright (Aleppo)

When the revolution began in Egypt, we were on Facebook giving Egyptians advice and sharing revolutionary songs. We felt like we were in Tahrir Square along with them.

And then the first demonstration occurred in Daraa. In Aleppo, I heard about it and wrote a Facebook status in support. I didn't hit "enter" to share it; I was too scared. My fingers were on the keyboard. I told myself that it was shameful that I was sharing things to support revolution in Egypt, but when the same things were happening in my own country, I was too afraid to do anything.

So I finally hit "enter." I went to bed sure that the regime's people were going to arrest me the next morning.

# Abu Tarek, engineer (rural Hama)

I called my friends in Daraa and asked them what was happening over there. We all felt moved. But what was the solution? What should we do?

In my village, we sit together in the evenings and play cards and chess. We talked with each other and decided: Friday, March 25. We should have a demonstration, going out from the biggest mosque in Hama.

The regime knew that something might happen, so it sent its people to calm things down. The former secretary for the local wing of the Baath Party was at the mosque. He'd been the secretary during the 1982 events. The imam invited him to speak to the crowd, and he said, "Nothing happened in Daraa. Everything you're hearing is lies."

People had accumulated so much anger over the years, pent-up anger that needed to be released. They started shouting, "Shut up! Don't tell us what to do! You're shameful and corrupt!" And then everyone got up and marched out of the mosque. We walked only three hundred meters before the security forces rushed into the crowd and started beating us.

The next Friday, the security forces started beating people while they were still inside the mosque. They didn't even give us the chance to leave. Despite that, the second demonstration was even bigger than the first. All of Hama was saying: We're going to march.

I have a cousin who didn't support protest. He'd say, "This isn't the right time. There's no preparation. We're not organized." My response was that the regime was going to prevent us from organizing forever. We weren't allowed to have a political party or a newspaper or a meeting. I had to get security clearance to invite fifteen people to my house to listen to someone tell stories.

The regime didn't want change. It was in control. It had five hundred thousand security force officers and the entire economy in its grip. At some point we had to confront it.

# Kareem, doctor (Homs)

March 18 was the first demonstration in Homs. Friday prayers ended and people marched out of the mosque, chanting. Security agents were waiting for them at the gate. They grabbed most of them and dragged them away on buses. The demonstration was immediately aborted.

The next Friday was March 25. My friends and I were drinking coffee together, as we did every Friday. We didn't think anything was going to happen. And then we started to hear a loud noise. *Hooooo!* It was people! We went down to the street. *Hoooo!* A huge number of people. They were marching from the old city toward downtown.

We couldn't believe it! Is it real? Others joined, and it grew and grew and became an enormous demonstration. I joined, too. The security forces were there, but were shocked and didn't know what to do.

People chanted for about three hours. Then busloads of regime supporters arrived, most of them Alawites. They threw stones and then both groups were throwing stones at each other. Security forces intervened. They shot tear gas and arrested a lot of people.

One of the protestors climbed the wall of the Military Officers' Club and tore down the picture of Hafez al-Assad. He stomped on the picture until he tore it to pieces. When this scene was broadcast on television, people couldn't believe their eyes.

Fridays passed and each demonstration was larger than the one the week before. If you came to Homs during the week you'd think that life was normal. Stores were open and people went to work. But the security forces had videos of the demonstrations and were arresting anyone who appeared in them.

On Fridays, security forces filled the main square downtown and set up checkpoints to prevent people from getting there. In response, every neighborhood started launching its own demonstration. Even people who don't normally pray would come to the mosques just to participate in the demonstration. Everyone had this thirst to do something. There was confidence that we could overthrow the president by peaceful protest alone.

## Ziyad, doctor (Homs)

Once, a young man entered one of the mosques in Homs. You could see a necklace around his neck, but the rest of it was tucked inside his shirt. He lined up and prayed with everyone else. And when he bowed, the necklace fell out. The pendant was a cross. People said to him, "Either you're wearing that necklace by mistake, or you came to the mosque by mistake." And the Christian young man said, "I came here to go out in the demonstration with all of you."

## Miriam, former student (Aleppo)

One Friday, my brother went to the mosque, where there was supposed to be a protest. As they finished the prayer, he thought to himself, "Why is it always someone else who starts the chanting? This time, I'm going to be the one!"

So he stood up and started chanting, "God is great!" And everyone just stared at him. It turned out that they had changed the location of the protest.

## Hadi, shop owner (rural Latakia)

In our village in Latakia, it started with graffiti. People went out at night and wrote on the walls in complete secrecy. We called them night bats. We'd wake up in the morning and see slogans like, "The people want the overthrow of the regime."

I actually had a paint store. The security forces came and told me that I needed to register every customer buying paint. I had to record the person's name, ID number, and the names of his father and mother. People got scared and stopped buying paint. Eventually I had to close the store. But the graffiti writers just got their paint from somewhere else and kept going.

Later, the phase of night chanting began. Electricity was cut daily at seven in the evening, so there were no lights. In the darkness, people would shout from their windows, "God is great!" Whoever was strong of heart would start, and then everyone else joined in. You'd hear voices coming from all directions. The security forces would arrive and everybody would go quiet. Then the security forces would leave and everyone would start again.

## Mahmoud, actor (Homs)

In the beginning, people were afraid to talk on the phone. So they'd speak in code. I was at school in Damascus and would call my mom, in Homs.

"Hey, Mom, what's new?"

"By God, today it's raining and foggy."

"Foggy" meant security forces were present. "Raining" meant they're shooting. "Storms" meant shelling. And we were saying all of this in the heat of summer!

I'd say, "Yeah, Mom, we have to put up with the weather."

I was too scared to protest. I went only once, because my girlfriend wanted to go. In the taxi and then at the demonstration, I thought that everyone else was a security agent about to arrest me.

A guy I know got arrested that way. They brought him in for interrogation, but he wouldn't confess that he'd gone to a protest. Then they showed him a video and asked, "If you didn't go, who is this?" He turned yellow. In the video he was in the middle of a demonstration, sitting on someone's shoulders—and that someone turned out to be the interrogator.

# Husayn, playwright (Aleppo)

Slowly protests got bigger. Some neighborhoods in Aleppo held demonstrations every week. I started working side by side with the young protesters. We organized weekly meetings in our houses, in secret, of course.

One day I was talking on the phone about going to a protest. My daughter was sixteen or seventeen at that time. She heard me and said, "I want to go with you to a demonstration."

I told her, "Do I look like someone who would go to a demonstration?"

She insisted, "You're telling someone that the wedding will be at two in the afternoon. Who has a wedding at that hour? You're talking about going to the demonstration, and I want to go with you!"

We argued about it, but in the end I agreed to let her come. She got ready and then her mom, my ex-wife, followed us to the door. She said, "If you two are going to protest, I'm going, too. I won't stay home alone."

After that, they both became addicted to protesting. We found out later that my daughter was even skipping school to attend activist meetings. So her mom started to take her to school every day and wait outside to walk her back home.

## Yasser, former student (Aleppo)

I went to my first protest in Aleppo in a big group, but there were so many people there that I lost my friends. I saw how the shabeeha looked. One was holding a cane and pretending to use it as a crutch, even though he wasn't limping. One of them had a tool and was underneath a car, acting like he was fixing something. They were all pretending to do things, but really had all of these objects so they could beat people. After a while, everyone was suspecting everyone else.

The protest was supposed to begin at 8:30. By 8:35, nothing had started. Then an old man passed by the guy who was responsible for starting the chanting. The old man asked, "Why are you just standing there? Either say something or leave."

The young guy said to himself, "If this old man is braver than me, I'm going to kill myself." So he went out. He started shouting. And then everyone else went out, too. Imagine you have a deck of cards and all the cards go flying everywhere. That's what it was like.

# Jamal, doctor (Hama)

It was impossible to get big numbers to demonstrate in Damascus. People were enormously afraid. So we'd mount "flash protests": We'd chant for just five minutes or so, and then run away.

People also came up with alternative ways of showing that they were against the regime. People would agree on a time and place, and then everyone would show up wearing the same color. For example, everyone would come to the same café, wearing black. Nobody would say a thing; it was just a way of showing the size of the opposition. Eventually the security forces figured out what was happening and came after people dressed in the designated color.[]

You know, if we'd listened to our parents, we never would have gone out at all. That generation lived through Hama. My aunt was pregnant at the time. My parents took her to the hospital. They had to stop at checkpoints on the way there and saw corpses lined along the road. My father carries that sight inside him until now. He still has that fear until this day. Whenever we watched anything on TV related to politics, he'd say, "Turn off the television!" He couldn't even bear to watch a political TV show—that's how afraid he was.

My generation is also afraid—but not like them. I now say to my father, "Why were you silent all of those years?" We say this to their entire generation.

## Rima, writer (Suwayda)

I was in a demonstration. Others were shouting and I joined them. I started to whisper, *Freedom.* And after that I started to hear myself repeating, *Freedom, freedom, freedom.* And then I started shouting, *Freedom!* My voice mingled with other voices. When I heard my voice I started shaking and crying. I felt like I was flying. I thought to myself, "This is the first time I have ever heard my own voice." I thought, "This is the first time I have a soul and I am not afraid of death or being arrested or anything else." I wanted to feel this freedom forever. And I told myself that I would never let anyone steal my voice again.

And after that day I started to join all the demonstrations.

## Amal, former student (Aleppo)

Students were in the courtyard of the university, waiting for class to start. Someone started shouting, "God is great!" And then others joined in and started chanting, "Freedom!" I got goosebumps. I was with a friend and she grabbed my purse to hold me back, but I moved forward to join the demonstration. It was like I wasn't in control of my own body, and my legs were just moving by themselves. My friend kept pulling my purse backward, and I kept moving forward. The purse strap broke, and I merged into the crowd.

## Sana, graphic designer (Damascus)

I was very scared on my way to the demonstration. It was night. We put scarves over our faces so the security forces couldn't recognize us and walked through narrow streets to the square. The square was lit and people were playing music, with drums and flute. I don't know who grabbed my hands from the left or from the right, but we started singing and dancing and jumping. It was a party to overthrow the regime. At that moment I didn't care about anything else. I was so happy. It was a moment that I will never forget for the rest of my life: the moment I stood together with strangers, dancing and shouting to overthrow Bashar.

My husband and I agreed that only one of us would go to protest at a time. One would go, and the other would stay home, just in case something happened. He went to a demonstration before I did, and came back home very emotional. He was crying: "Anyone who doesn't live this moment cannot consider himself alive." When I came back from my first demonstration, he asked me how it was. I told him that he was right.

## Shadi, accountant (rural Hama)

My first demonstration was better than my wedding day. And when my wife heard me say that, she refused to talk to me for a month.

# Waddah, graduate (Latakia)

My younger brother and I grew up in the Gulf and went back to Syria for school. To be honest, we hated Syrians a little. We felt that they had no problem being humiliated or abused. Sometimes I felt like I didn't even want to be Syrian. I just wanted to finish university and leave the country.

On March 21, I woke up in our apartment in Muadamiyah. I heard, "Freedom, freedom." I thought I was still asleep and said to myself, "I wish I could just stay dreaming." But it turned out that the voices were coming from outside. I opened my door and yelled, "Demonstration!" I banged on my housemate's door and yelled, "Demonstration! Demonstration!" Then I realized that I was barefoot and in my pajamas. I got dressed and ran outside.

My brother came outside and joined me. I told him, "Go back home!" I felt responsible for him and was afraid that he'd get hurt. He didn't listen to me, of course. It was a revolution; nobody listened to anyone anymore.

I started yelling in a loud voice, "Dignity!" What did we want after dignity? We didn't know. But we knew that we needed more than just food.

The demonstration grew to about thirty people. Then these large men crowded around us. They were wearing black coats and were using cell phones. My brother and I escaped through the back streets. Everyone else in the demonstration got arrested. Everyone.

We both had long hair at the time, so we were recognizable. People were talking: "The two guys with the hair, where did they go?" But the people of Muadamiyah stood with us. Nobody reported where we were.

On March 25, we were hoping there would be another protest. My friend went to the mosque in Douma, and I went to the mosque in Muadamiyah. We figured out how to communicate: He'd text me a plus sign if there was a demonstration where he was, and a minus if the prayer finished and everybody just went home.

I was in the mosque, waiting for the plus. The imam kept talking and talking; it seemed like his sermon would never finish. Then I got a text: It was a plus. From the street, I heard people chanting, "With soul and blood, we sacrifice for you, Daraa!" We ran outside, jumping down the stairs in excitement.

We got to the street and found about two thousand people demonstrating. I started to cry. I was sorry that I had rejected my nationality. I was sorry that I had insulted these people and said that they were cowards. I thought, "I'm sorry, I'm so sorry. You are my brothers. You are my people. You are extraordinary."

# Annas, doctor (Ghouta)

The "Great Friday" demonstration was held in solidarity with Easter, out of respect for our Christian brothers. We wanted to encourage Christian Syrians to come out and participate.

We were a huge gathering of more than one hundred thousand people. People came from all over the Damascus suburbs: from Douma, Harasta, Zamalka, Kafr Batna . . . I remember we crossed a bridge and it trembled underneath our feet because we were so many people.

We reached Jobar and regime forces were there waiting for us. They fired tear gas and we retreated. Cars filled with police and shabeeha came from every direction and attacked with anything they could get their hands on. Because I'm a doctor, I tried to help whenever someone was injured. People were choking on tear gas and we'd pour cola on their faces, which counters the effect of gas. Their faces were sticky and glistening.

We'd been chanting, "Freedom, freedom, freedom!" And then someone shouted, "The people want the overthrow of the regime!" Everyone went silent. This was the first time we'd heard people say that.

No one spoke for ten to fifteen seconds. Honestly, we

were afraid that he could be part of the secret police. Everyone looked at each other and thought, "This guy just said what we've been wanting to say for years." After all those years of silence, we were hearing those words. We thought, "Do we chant with him or remain silent?" Everyone looked around, our faces pondering the unspoken. Do we speak or not?

## Cherin, mother (Aleppo)

We had gotten used to oppression. It was part of our life, like air, sun, water. We didn't even feel it. Like there is air, but you never ask, "Where is the air?" A lot of people were opposed to the way things were, but no one protested. You just adapted to oppression and rotted along with it.

And then—in one second, in one shout, one voice—you blow it up. You defy it and stand in front of death. You have an inheritance, and after thirty years, you slam it on the ground and shatter it.

I encouraged my sister's children to come with me to demonstrations. I felt that if they didn't try that experience, they'd be missing the real meaning of life. Even if the revolution failed, those days will never be forgotten. We'll tell our children that we took a stand. We went out. We spoke out. We shouted.

My sister's children, two girls and a boy, at first their voices were timid and low. But every time they repeated the chant, their voices got louder. The sound rose until you heard it echo between the buildings. All the people living in the buildings came out to see what was going on. Words can't describe what it was like.

Don't even imagine that it was easy to go out to a demonstration. No amount of courage allows you to stand and watch someone who has a gun and is about to kill you. We—as a people—were certain that they were going to kill us. Fear didn't go away because we knew that there was death.

But still, this incredible oppression made a young man or a young woman go out and say, "God is great!" And when those words are said, you and two hundred other people are ready to call out, "The people want the downfall of the regime!" Your voice gets louder and you feel intense feelings: You shudder and your body rises and everything you imagined just comes out. Tears come down. Tears of joy, because I broke the barrier . . . I am not afraid, I am a free being. Tears come down and your voice gets hoarse. Sadness and happiness and fear and courage . . . they're all mixed together in that voice, and it comes out very strong.

Before the revolution, I thought that Syria was for Assad. Syria was just the place where I lived, but it didn't belong to me. When the revolution began, I discovered that Syria was my country. As Kurds, we had thought that we were oppressed and others were favored by the regime. After the revolution we discovered that we were all suffering from the same oppression. We discovered that we had not been working together, and that is how the regime was able to dominate us.

## Abdul Rahman, engineer (Hama)

My parents were divorced and I was raised by a single mom. She had only a high school diploma and we were poor. Studying was my only hope for the future.

I always wanted to be an engineer, and I got a scholarship to study in Algeria. My mother sold a necklace she had received from her mother to buy me a plane ticket. As a teenager, I'd been a troublemaker. But when I found myself alone in Algeria, I became a serious student. I learned French and fell in love with an Algerian girl and became ranked first in the whole department.

I was finishing my master's degree when the Arab Spring started. Our dreams became so near. I was too afraid even to like the Syrian Revolution Facebook page, so I created another Facebook account under the name "Syrian Man," so I could participate freely. There was another Syrian guy with me in Algeria, but his family was in the Syrian police and loyal to Assad. When I showed him my political opinions, I felt like I was signing my death warrant. Later, one of his friends was killed in a demonstration. I showed him videos of the incident and said, "See the police? Maybe your cousins were involved in this." He was in shock.

I finished my exams and booked the first flight back to

Syria. From the Damascus airport, I got a taxi to the bus station. I couldn't wait to chat with someone about the revolution. I nearly said something to the taxi driver, forgetting all about the fact that many taxi drivers are security agents. Thank God, light from outside hit his arm and I saw a very big tattoo saying, "Praise Ali, Praise Bashar." Ali is a holy person for Shia, so this indicated that he considered Bashar to be a holy person, like a god. I shut my mouth.

I reached Hama at 6:30 in the morning and went out in a demonstration the same day. I felt like I was in heaven. My first shout was, "Death before humiliation!" Everything was happy. Even the stones of the street were happy. I could feel it coming from everywhere. People joined from all directions and the streets moved under our weight as we marched to al-Asi Square in the city center. Women threw rice and candies from the balconies. A sound system played the revolutionary song: "Oh shame / Oh shame / And you, son of my country, killing my children / Oh what a shame."

I felt like a free person. I thought, "I'm glad that I'm here at this moment. I'm glad that I belong to this place."

# Marcell, activist (Aleppo)

I used to be the Christian girl who talked about how everything is fine in Syria because the regime is secular and minorities have privileges. Then in 2005 I joined an online group and started to blog. Some guys I knew got arrested because of their online writing. That's when the issue began to have a face for me.

My first blog about the revolution was on March 15. I said that we deserved freedom. I never wrote under a fake name. That was risky, but I wanted all Syrians to know my identity: I'm a woman. And I'm Christian. And I believe that this regime should go. I don't see Muslims as people who kill Christians. I trust you. Let's go forward, together.

By April I was out in the street. I was living this divided life: I'd go out to protest, but I couldn't tell anyone. My family was supportive, but some friends were repeating what they heard on television about gangs destroying the country. I started to take people I know with me to protest. Jesus said, "Come and see." I believed that if more people had come to see demonstrations, things could have gone differently.

Demonstrations were amazing. There were so many heroes—heroes who never knew how heroic they were.

Amazing people who took huge risks just to spread leaflets or to bring someone to the hospital. I also did crazy things to rescue total strangers, things that could have gotten me killed. Because we were together, shouting for the same goals.

During that period, my mother was crying all the time. I wanted her to accept the reality that I might die. I didn't want to feel like I had special privileges; that my parents were going to send me to Europe to wait until the revolution was over. If other people were going to get beaten in the streets, I was going to get beaten in the streets. And if they were going to prison, then I was going to prison.

The security forces started calling me to come for weekly interrogations. I'd go to interrogation in the morning and protest at night. I was sleeping at friends' houses because it became too dangerous to spend the night at home.

I started to see my mother less and less. One day I came home to visit. She was going to a wedding that evening. On her way back, the car stopped at a checkpoint and troops opened fire by accident. She was shot and killed immediately.

It was at the hospital that I realized I was no longer a normal person. My sister was crying, but I couldn't grieve normally. Some very close friends didn't even come to visit at the hospital, because they were afraid that the security forces would arrest them there. The odd thing was, they were regime supporters. The more someone supported the regime, the more he was scared of it.

I started to think. The revolutionary activists were going to hear that my mother died. They'd say that the regime killed her, and she is a martyr, and they would want to come to the church to pay their respects. I didn't want there to be conflict with the congregation, so I met with other activists. I told them that I wanted everyone to wear white T-shirts and carry red roses. No slogans. No chants. We want to do something that Christians would understand, and something peaceful that reflected the revolution itself. I told them to trust me on this. If they came and shouted slogans, the people at the church would get scared. And then the regime would come and beat the protesters, and people would think that it was justified because the protestors had started it.

In the end, almost five hundred people attended the funeral. They came into the church silently and peacefully, just as I'd asked. There were security forces nearby, but they couldn't come shoot people in church, simply because they were holding red roses.

It was amazing. I respected how all the activists wanted to shout against Bashar al-Assad. But they saw how impressed these ordinary civilians were with them. One person from the church said to me, "God bless you. What you managed to do peacefully today was really important." I didn't know how strong I was. Having to hold that message, in that situation. I had the courage even to make my mom's death a revolutionary statement.

Part IV

# CRACKDOWN

# Miriam, former student (Aleppo)

If Bashar had only come out in his first speech and said, "I am with you, my people. I want to help you and be with you step by step," I can guarantee you one million percent that he would have been the greatest leader in the Arab world. He had that kind of potential. Instead, he assumed that the Syrian people love him, that they don't understand anything, and that they'll follow him no matter what. But we weren't as foolish as the government thought we were.

## Jamal, doctor (Hama)

I was working at the hospital when Bashar delivered his first speech after the demonstrations began. All the doctors and nurses and other staff gathered to watch it on TV.

There were probably fifty of us. We were very hopeful. But he showed no understanding at all of the people's demands and the reasons for the protests. He said, "If you want war, we are ready for war." He actually laughed out loud. And then he abruptly ended his address, saying, "As-salamu alaykum—Goodbye."

We couldn't believe what we were hearing. There were even some regime supporters in the room, and they were shocked, too. It became painfully clear: This person should not be ruling us. He is too stupid to deserve to be our president.

# Tayseer, lawyer (Daraa)

On April 24 they laid siege to Daraa city. They surrounded the city and used airplanes to survey it. Then they attacked from different fronts, using all kinds of weapons: artillery, tanks, missiles. They cut water, electricity, and communications.

Soldiers would raid houses and spill the cooking oil on the floor. They'd spoil the food that people had stored in their winter pantries so they had nothing to eat. They'd shoot at water tanks so there was no water left.

They took over the main public hospital. If they put their hands on any injured person, it would be the end of him. So people started to treat the wounded in private homes instead. The dead were left in the streets, and people put them in warehouse coolers normally used for storing fruit and vegetables.

They positioned snipers that shot at anything that moved, even animals. They divided the city into grids and checkpoints. They cut off travel within the city to kill any sort of social life. This whole city was frozen. The atmosphere was one of complete terror. Imagine the children who experienced this. What social and psychological problems will those children face in the future?

They maintained a curfew for thirteen days. After that, people were allowed out for an hour or two a day. I was wanted by the police and stayed in another house so they wouldn't find and arrest me. It was only after curfew was lifted that I learned that they'd raided my home. They destroyed everything and arrested my son, my two brothers, and my four nephews.

My son was in prison for six months. He was tortured severely. We resorted to bribes and finally were able to get him released. Imprisoning people became an extortion trade. Those whose parents were able to pay got out. Those who couldn't stayed in prison and were done for.

## Abdel-Samed, business owner (rural Daraa)

The regime brought in forces to destroy Daraa completely. All of the neighboring villages held demonstrations that Friday, which we called "the Friday of Breaking the Siege." The regime arrested everyone there. Buses were filled with detainees. Only those who could run away managed to escape arrest.

Later, they returned the body of Hamza al-Khatib.[*] He's a cousin of mine and looks just like my son. He'd been tortured. They didn't leave any spot on his body without cigarette burns. His body was full of stab marks and his neck was broken. They'd cut off his genitals.

His mutilated corpse arrived and people saw what the regime had done to him. And that's when they realized that the regime was finished. There was no more trust. A delegation had gone to meet with the president, and he had promised that he would address their concerns. Instead he sent them this present. It was a way of telling them, "Either you be quiet, or we will do this to you."

---

[*]   Hamza al-Khatib was a thirteen-year-old who was killed in regime custody. After videos and photographs of his mutilated body circulated widely online and in the media, he became regarded as a symbol of the Syrian revolution.

Before this, people had some hope that the regime might listen to their demands and try to make reforms. After Hamza, people realized that the regime is on one side and the people are on another. That's it. The only thing our leaders know how to do is kill, kill, kill, kill, and kill. And after that, kill again. Kill anyone. It doesn't matter if he's a civilian or a child.

The regime went even further in terrorizing us. It said, "We won't just kill you. We'll kill your entire family, too." I've heard that in some countries the government only arrests the wanted person himself, not his brother or mother or sister. In Syria, the entire family and the entire neighborhood is accused and targeted.

# Adam, media organizer (Latakia)

The regime dealt with each region in Syria differently. In some places, they tried soft politics. In other places, like Latakia, they went extreme from the very beginning. It was a manipulative, evil way of doing business.

One night I woke up to heavy shooting. Being the idiot I am, I got in my car and went to trace the source of the shooting. I got to this huge square in Latakia and found all these shabeeha. Shabeeha were the only ones armed at that time, apart from the security forces and the army. They were civilian, most likely Alawites, working for somebody connected to the Assad family or other influential families. They did whatever they wanted and nobody dared to stop them.

So I reached the shabeeha, and they're all sitting there, shooting in the air. It's four o'clock in the morning and they're blasting pro-Assad songs. Many of them were drunk or just being stupid. But they couldn't have gone out and started shooting without authorization. So there was a purpose. The regime wanted to say, "We're still in control and if you try anything we'll break your face."

They were celebrating in an Alawite neighborhood. After ten or fifteen minutes, they went to one of the biggest squares in a Sunni neighborhood. They went as this huge convoy, waking everybody up, shooting in the air, playing the songs. These huge guys, on steroids, with guns, just showing off. As if to say, "Don't even think that what's going on in other places is going to happen here."

The next day was the first demonstration in Latakia. After Friday prayers, people shouted, "Daraa, we're with you!" There was nothing about the government or the regime. Riot police came and cracked down.

I heard gunfire. I don't know who was shooting, but I'm pretty sure it was the shabeeha. They were filled with rage. A big reason why was that rumors were circulating that jihadists from all over the world were coming to behead Alawites. I heard the rumors, too, because I was living in an Alawite neighborhood. You know, many Alawites hated the Assad regime, and I think the regime knew that. They also know that the Alawite community is their lifeline, their base for survival.

So from day one, the regime was saying that groups of radicals were coming. It was like, "Imagine what will happen to you if one of those terrorists get into power." Alawites felt that they had no choice but to be 100 percent behind the leadership. And Bouthaina Shaaban, the regime spokesperson, got on TV and said, "Those radicals, they want to make strife between the Shia and blah blah blah." Are you kidding me? Our children are in prison and we have a shitty government and you're talking about Shia and Sunnis? I didn't even know the difference between Shiite and Sunni until this whole thing started, because nobody cared. Don't get me wrong—Shia and Sunnis have been fighting forever. But nobody was mentioning any of that in Syria at the time. In 2011, the needs, the goals, and the demands had nothing to do with that. The goals were political reform, participation, real representation, and some actual active citizenship in the country.

The people in power saw those goals as a fundamental threat to their grip over the country. The only way they could maintain full control was by reframing the argument from reform to Shia and Sunnis and radicals. They implemented that policy through their political speeches and military approach. And they imposed it on the ground through all those things that they used shabeeha for: burning Qurans, going into mosques, etcetera. Those were the tools that they used to reframe the argument. And eventually things ended up where we are now.

There is another event that I still remember. One night, people started shouting from their balconies, "Freedom, freedom! God is great!" They were just shouting and banging on pots and pans. There was an army detail on the street. The soldiers formed a circle, with the officer in the middle. They faced outward, pointing their machine guns all over the place. I served in the military so I know this formation. It's what you do when enemies are coming at you from all sides or when you don't know where the enemy is. This formation is your last stand.

So they thought that they were surrounded by enemies. And they were in their own city. And nothing was happening except that people were shouting.

The regime was basically doing everything possible to put sects against each other and create a toxic environment, where nobody trusts anybody and nobody knows who's in control. Every side had its own enemy. For Alawites, the enemy was extremist radicals. For Sunnis, it was the shabeeha. For the soldier on the streets, it was the Israelis or whoever they were told that they were fighting. And this is what made things escalate. It was literally being pushed by the regime and the forces connected to it.

## Kareem, doctor (Homs)

On April 16, there was a vigil in Homs. An officer came to clear it, but people didn't respond. He started shooting, and seventeen people were killed. People moved the casualties to the hospital where I was working. The scene was unlike anything I'd ever seen in my life.

The next day there was a funeral for the martyrs. Thousands and thousands of people participated. When the funeral ended, people wanted to do something. So they started shouting, "To the square! To the square!" It was a spontaneous reaction. There was so much anger. The crowd turned around and walked toward Clock Square, in the center of the city.

People gathered and more people joined. All the shops closed. People set up tents and ate and drank. They chanted and delivered speeches. Night came and people decided to sleep there. There was a feeling: This is an opportunity that we should not lose. This is our square and we should stay here until the regime falls.

Security forces gathered near the sit-in and decided to storm it. Negotiations were ongoing between the regime and some representatives of the people. And here the regime betrayed us. I was at home in bed about three kilometers away. I woke up to a sound that I thought was heavy rain. I went to the window and realized it was bullets.

Security forces were attacking the square. People were being slaughtered. I called the hospital and asked them to send me an ambulance. What I saw on the road from my house to the square was extraordinary: All of Homs was on the streets. People didn't know what was happening. They were running, afraid.

Security forces opened fire on the ambulance, so it wasn't possible to move a single injured person. Only one or two wounded people managed to escape and make it to the hospital. We just sat there and waited and cried. There was nothing we could do. People were dying and we couldn't even reach them to offer first aid.

The next morning, people saw that the square had been hosed down with water. There was no trace of anything whatsoever. They took away the people and removed all traces of the crime. The only thing that remained was the bullet holes on the buildings.

This was the turning point in Homs. After that, people felt that there was no going back to the way things were. Before there was a 50 percent chance of no return. Now it became 150 percent.

## Abdel-Samed, business owner (rural Daraa)

In the beginning, things were spontaneous. People were just angry. Later, we saw that people needed to get organized.

Coordination started from the second week. Leading figures in the community, and anyone with drive and an eagerness to contribute, gathered together. They divided themselves into groups to deal with specific tasks. Some worked in media. Some organized demonstrations, figuring out where and when they'd be held. Some wrote the speeches that were delivered at demonstrations. Some worked on slogans—demonstrations were being shown on TV to the entire world, so we needed to send the right message. Some secured the sound system; we only had one in town, so it was crucial that people hide the stereo speakers so the security forces couldn't confiscate them. Some people provided security for demonstrations. The thinking was, if the regime attacks, how do we minimize the number of martyrs?

Each village started having meetings. At the same time, we communicated with people in other towns and villages who were doing the same thing. So we all got to know each other.

# Ibrahim, former student (rural Hama)

In every neighborhood, someone took charge of chanting, someone made signs, someone took photographs, etcetera. Some people would be stationed at the entrances of the neighborhood during demonstrations; as soon as they saw police coming, they'd tell everyone else to escape.

We'd film demonstrations, upload the video, distribute it, and then delete everything so we'd have nothing on us if we got caught. We used protest names in our communications with each other. That way, if someone was arrested and was forced to report on the others, he couldn't reveal anyone's real identity.

At first, each province had a different name for demonstrations. Then people started coordinating to choose one name for all of Syria. That made protest more powerful and meaningful.

Women didn't go out to protest in Hama in the beginning. But after a while they came out, too, and played a major role. There was a seamstress who sewed flags for us.* If the regime caught her, they would have slaughtered

---

* By late 2011, the protest movement had distanced itself from the Assad regime by adopting the flag that Syria had used after

her. She refused to take any money for her work. She also knew calligraphy, so she would draw beautiful banners. One guy would pick them up and hide them somewhere that only the neighborhood activists knew about. They wouldn't leave them in anyone's homes because the whole family would be in danger if they were discovered.

---

independence. The opposition flag, which had a green band and red stars, stood in contrast to the state flag, which had a red band and green stars.

## Abu Tha'ir, engineer (Daraa)

During the first few days of the revolution, we weren't careful, and we brought the wounded to government-run hospitals. In the morning, we'd take an injured person to the hospital with a gunshot wound in his leg. That night, we'd return to find him dead with a gunshot to the head. Guys would die and they'd force their families to say that their sons had been killed by terrorist gangs.

So we created field hospitals. A friend of mine donated his house and transformed it into a place to help the wounded. There were doctors and nurses, and young women and men volunteered to help. If the regime caught them, it would kill them.

Sometimes when people arrived they were already dead. Sometimes people would die in front of us, and we couldn't do anything because we didn't have bandages to stop the bleeding. Sometimes someone died at night and we couldn't bury him until the morning. Because of the electricity cuts, we might not have ice to put on his body. The smell would be terrible.

There was a man called Jaber and his mission was to go around and find ice from other people in the city. He had a motorcycle and sometimes would travel long distances, searching for ice. And then Jaber was killed, and we couldn't find any ice for him.

## Beshr, student (Damascus)

We formed our neighborhood coordination committee. They cut the Internet at that time, and we started to get satellite Internet. I was asked to hide the satellite phone for our neighborhood. That was so dangerous that I couldn't take that decision alone, so I asked every member of my family if they agreed to have the phone in our house. Everyone agreed.

Twice, activists sent me satellite phones to deliver to other activists. I didn't know the real names of the person who was giving me the phone or the person to whom I delivered the phone. They didn't know my real name, either. The guy who gave me phones was supposed to email me anytime before he called me. Once he called me without prior notification and told me to meet him in ten minutes. I wasn't sure what to do. I phoned an activist friend, but she didn't answer. I decided to go and was just stepping out when she called back. She said, "Be careful, this man was detained a week ago—they might be using his phone to trap you." I asked another friend to go check on the meeting place. He went and found six security guards waiting.

My mom had always been really rigid about our studies.

Once I overheard her talking to my grandma. Grandma said, "Your son isn't focusing. He's a senior in high school now, and exams are coming up." Mom said, "I understand, but I can't let him down. I keep remembering how his father went to prison. We need to continue the struggle." I felt so supported. I was like, "Wow! I love you, Mom!"

Some time after that, the security forces came looking for me. I hid in a back room. My mom opened the door a crack and said, "I can't let you in because I'm alone and not wearing a headscarf." I panicked, trying to think about how I could climb out a window or something. But my mom just coolly told them that I was studying at a friend's house and that she could not allow them inside. The officers said that I should call them, and then went away. Mom was so calm the whole time. I have no idea how.

# Ayham, web developer (Damascus)

There was a systematic effort to give the movement a bad image. Every time a demonstration passed by a street, the police would run after it and break windows and lights, or sometimes spray paint graffiti. On YouTube you can find a lot of videos of them doing this. At the same time, the regime would show these images of destroyed property on TV and say, "*This* is the freedom they want. The freedom to destroy the country, the freedom to disrespect religions, etcetera."

We always faced this question: "What is the freedom you're calling for?" So we tried to define freedom. Slowly, individual efforts came together. My brother was in a co-ordination committee at his university and they were very creative with computer stuff. They started some YouTube channels where they produced videos about the main things that people wanted. They said: We wanted freedom of speech. We wanted release of political prisoners because we knew that they were potential leaders. We wanted to get rid of the Eighth Amendment to the constitution, which says that the Baath Party is the ruling party of the state. Because the freedom to form political parties wouldn't mean much if the Baath Party always controlled the presidency and a majority in the parliament.

We faced other questions, like: "What's the alternative to the regime? If not Assad, who can take his place?" They're stupid questions. Everybody who opened their mouths to talk about what was happening in the country was shoved in prison. The regime puts all the movement leaders in prison, and then comes and says that the movement has no leaders. Well, how do you expect there to be leaders when you arrest them all?

# Mustafa, barber (Salamiyah)

I'm from Salamiyah and a member of the Ismaili sect, which is a branch of Shiite Islam. Ismailis have been persecuted across history. Personally, I'm an atheist and a Marxist. But as a barber, I deal with people with all sorts of different opinions.

We started establishing local coordination committees. These put the appropriate people in the appropriate places. Age and education and social class weren't important. This is a major indicator that the Syrian people are not backward. They're ready for democratic life. As Marxists, we always dreamed about this situation when people would govern themselves, from the bottom up, without hierarchy.

The regime didn't want to admit that they were fighting any sort of secular entity. So when we started having big demonstrations, it drove the regime crazy. Salamiyah had a big effect on all of Syria. It raised people's awareness that government propaganda wasn't true. Daraa, a predominantly Sunni city, was demonstrating. And Baniyas, a mixed city, was demonstrating. And Salamiyah, a city of minorities known for its leftist tendencies, was demonstrating. Everyone had the same slogans, the same political principles, the same demands for freedom. It wasn't

Salafis or foreign agents challenging the regime. It was a revolution.

For forty years the regime had been working on segregating people by religion. People from Salamiyah are from a minority and people from Hama are from the majority religion, so they're supposed to hate each other. But when Hama was bombarded, people started fleeing by the thousands, and we welcomed them into our homes.

After months, the regime launched a big raid on Salamiyah. People were arrested from the streets and from their homes. Fifteen of us escaped to the areas around Damascus. These areas have a strong Islamic culture. People are religious, but they opened their doors to us from minority communities. The respect they showed was unbelievable. We'd go to demonstrations, and local people would put us in the middle of the crowd so we'd be safer when security forces started shooting.

## Musa, professor (Aleppo)

In general, the regime focused on the cities and created a huge security presence that made it very difficult to protest. It was also easy to recruit people there to work as spies. For example, there were suddenly street vendors all over Aleppo. They were paid shabeeha, especially the watermelon vendors. They were armed with knives and their role was to attack protests as soon as they broke out. The result was that sometimes there would be hundreds of protesters followed by hundreds of arrests. Or sometimes the regime would learn about an upcoming protest and let it happen, just so they could gather information about who was involved.

Also, in big cities, not everyone knows each other. Young guys would be chased by the police, and they'd be afraid to escape into just any shop, because the owner might be a regime agent. In the countryside, everyone knows everyone else. People could flee more easily. And they could organize by word of mouth and protest for an hour or two before the security forces even got there.

# Ghayth, former student (Aleppo)

During the peak of demonstrations at the University of Aleppo, women played a huge role. Women who wore headscarves would hide papers and signs in their long coats, because they wouldn't get searched. The male dorms had so many demonstrations that the authorities closed them down. Only female dorms remained open, so women took charge of organizing, and then would pass information on to the guys. If the security forces attacked male demonstrators, women would stand in their way; at that time, security officers saw touching women as a red line. A lot of women really came to the rescue.

So many people were imprisoned, we thought about doing something for their families. Even simple things, like buying milk for children. We considered prisoners' families to be like our own families; it was our duty to help them. My brother got active in this. Once someone saw him make a delivery and then reported him to the intelligence services. He was brought in for interrogation twice—and this after he'd already spent a month in prison for demonstrating. So he took his wife and children and left the country.

# Ayham, web developer (Damascus)

Damascus was extremely controlled. You could see secret police everywhere. It was like that guy on *Game of Thrones* who has those birds, as he calls them. But the beautiful thing for us, the mesmerizing thing, was that at some point we stopped giving a shit. We were afraid, but we were just too excited. You've been suppressed for so long and suddenly the lid comes off. The idea of being able to speak was captivating.

Everybody said that the regime would collapse during the month of Ramadan, because instead of gathering at the mosque for prayer only on Fridays, people gathered every night. The atmosphere was pumped with energy.

The twenty-seventh of Ramadan is a holy day, and people stay up all night praying and reading the Quran. Every year over five thousand people gathered at the mosque near our house. Volunteers from the neighborhood helped prepare a meal for people to eat before sunrise. I don't pray, but I always participated in preparing the meal, because I thought it was a beautiful social event.

People started arriving. There were a lot of old people, but also guys with body piercings and strange haircuts. You could see that they had no idea what to do. Some guys were wearing shorts, which you aren't supposed to do in a mosque. Out of respect, they were trying to pull their shorts down toward their ankles. But that exposed their backsides. It was a beautiful scene of the complex social fabric that we had in Damascus.

Thousands of security officers surrounded the mosque. It looked like a scene from King Arthur. They were just standing there with sticks and shields and angry faces. We were arranging the food and had a long argument about whether to bring meals to the officers outside. A lot of people said no, they don't deserve it. Others said it was a gesture to show we meant no harm. They were young soldiers. People like us, basically, doing their military service.

Three or four brave guys took boxes filled with meals to the commanding officer. They said, "We come in peace. This is for you because you're standing here all night." The officer responded, "Take this back inside or I'll kill you."

The prayers started and the imam said, "God protect us from those who harm us." People started shouting, "Amen! Amen!" It's a religious word and the majority of people there knew nothing about religion. But you could see them crying and shivering. I don't believe in prayer, but I believe in the emotional charge that prayer carries. You know what it's like, when you believe in a cause and you're standing with people who also believe in it? And you're surrounded by threat and you can feel the fear?

Prayer ended. Silence. Then one person shouted, "Freedom!" Others stood up and started shouting their lungs out. Old people grabbed their shoes and fled.

And then: chaos. Everything turned into a battle. The soldiers started throwing rocks. And that's when we realized our big mistake: Someone had donated juice for the meal, and it was in glass bottles. People started throwing bottles at the officers. You could hear glass shattering.

The regime had snipers all around and one guy in the courtyard got shot in the head. People rushed back inside and police ran in behind them. Some people were on the second-floor balcony. If they got caught they were going to get arrested or killed. So they started jumping down or hanging on to the curtains. Everything got destroyed.

Inside, we got word that Damascus's big imams were negotiating with the chief of police. The sun came up and eventually they said it was safe to leave. We opened the door and saw policemen chanting, "Assad! Assad!" They told us that the area in front of the mosque was secure. But the moment we crossed the street, the officers started chasing us. I ran like I'd never run before.

## Abu Firas, fighter (rural Idlib)

My brother was kidnapped by the shabeeha. After eighteen days, they sent him back to us, killed under torture.

You can't imagine how he died. His toenails were ripped out. His bones had been pierced with a drill. There were marks from being beaten and burned. His nose was beaten so severely that it was flat.

We buried him. And about three months later, some guys who were released from prison contacted us and told us that my brother was actually still alive. They'd been with him in prison. The body we'd buried belonged to a different person; he was so disfigured that we couldn't tell he was someone else.

# Shafiq, graduate (Daraya)

Twenty-two of us were in charge of organizing demonstrations in Daraya. Of them, only three are still around
today. We'd all contribute about $20 to buy flags or ma-
terials to make posters. We'd plan on Wednesdays and
Thursdays, and protest on Fridays.

In late May, the security forces attacked Daraya. They
cut off phone lines, cell phone service, and Internet.
They raided houses, taking all the young men they found.
So it became absolutely necessary for my brothers and
me to leave our house. We started hiding in agricultural
fields.

We stopped protesting on Fridays to avoid clashing with
the security forces. At the end of the day, security officers
are our brothers; we didn't want bloodshed. Instead of
demonstrations, we organized other peaceful activities to
show the government that we were still there. We'd write
on the walls. One night we held a candlelight vigil.

Then the regime besieged the city again. They charged
into our house at three in the morning. Officers wrecked
the house and cursed my mom and dad, saying that they
were looking for their terrorist sons.

We went back to planning. One night after a meeting my
brother went back home. Security forces were waiting there

and arrested him. After that, they started calling my dad and telling him that they'd let my brother go if he turned me in. I stopped going home as much as possible.

A guy I knew let me stay at his house. One morning, there was a knock at the door. It was the security forces. I ran out the backdoor and tried to hide, but one of the officers spotted me. Until then I'd been really proud that I'd never been captured. I was devastated that I got caught.

They took me to be interrogated, beating me every step of the way. At the interrogation center, they made us take off all our clothes. They mocked us and spat on us, but it was actually more dignifying than humiliating. You didn't do anything but say, "Freedom," and that was enough to rattle the entire regime and make them panic. For me, that was victory.

Later I was thrown in a cell. I kept telling myself to be strong, that I was doing this for a cause and that God would be with my mother, who now had two sons in prison. To the general public, whoever is arrested is considered dead until he's released.

In the cell, you'd hear the sounds of other people being tortured. People screaming and screaming. Interrogators used three different bells for the torture rooms, and we were there long enough to recognize each of them. One bell was for the room with "the tire."* Another was for the room with electric cables. The third bell was for the room with the most extreme form of torture, where they don't kill you but almost do and leave you wishing you were dead.

The door to the corridor was metal and it made this loud noise you know from the movies. Every time you heard it, you thought, "It must be my turn." And all the others thought, "It must be my turn." Everyone was scared. The noises were harder than the torture itself. Sound enters you in a different way. It felt like the sounds themselves were killing you.

One day the bell rang for the worst kind of torture, and that time they came for me. The sixty seconds it took to drag me down the hallway were the hardest part of my entire imprisonment. It felt like a year before they threw me into a room. I was blindfolded, but heard the tap of shoes circling me. The interrogator didn't utter a word. After about fifteen minutes, I couldn't take it anymore. I said, "I'll confess to whatever you want. Just ask me something!" Then I collapsed on the floor.

---

* A form of torture in which a person is bent at the waist, forced to stick his torso and legs through a car tire, and beaten.

That's when the interrogator started beating me. I felt relieved to hear him, finally. He stuffed me into a car tire and was counting lashes until like fifty-seven. Then he counted "sixty" instead of "fifty-eight," and said, "Oh no, we messed up, we need to start over." He started hitting me with the electric cable, emptying the whole cable into my body from my toenails to my chest. Sensitive areas, too. I was beyond feeling. At that point, you lose your mind.

After interrogation, I was transferred to a group cell. Fifty-two prisoners were in a space two by four meters. It was too crowded for all of us to lie down at the same time, so we'd take turns sleeping and standing. Everyone was afraid of everyone else: Someone might go in for torture and spill everything you told him. It turned out that one of the guys in our cell was planted there to gather information.

Life became routine. One beating in the morning and another in the evening. You go, you get beaten, you return. We got to use the bathroom twice a day. You had until the count of ten to run in and out; if you didn't finish in time, you got hit. We worked together to share food, because there was never enough. Everyone in the cell was equal: the engineer, the doctor, whoever. It was beautiful, in a way. But also sad. We young guys would try to take beatings for the older ones.

At some point I forgot what my parents looked like.

Sometimes I'd start thinking about all those people who had disappeared over the years and we didn't even notice. Sometimes I cursed everyone over fifty. Why were you quiet and let them rule us? Once I'd seen a program on National Geographic about a monkey. Every time he climbed a tree to get a banana, they'd hit him and he'd go back down. They kept doing it, again and again. The other monkeys saw and none even dared to climb the tree. They started eating dirt, even though the banana tree was right there. After a month, just seeing the banana was enough to make the monkey terrified.

My dad never mentioned the Hama massacre. He was too afraid; maybe a government informant would find out and they'd kill the whole family. In 2006, Syria got the Internet. We read about the Hama massacre, the political prisoners . . . We, the new generation, became aware of how terrible the regime is. We wanted to know why we couldn't have the banana and we reached the point where we just had to go for it. We thought everything would be great, but it turned out that the banana was booby-trapped. It blew up in our faces.

After ninety days in prison, I was brought to court. Everyone there was clean and well dressed, and I looked like a caveman, with my hair grown long and wild. The judge was sympathetic and let me go. They unshackled me and I returned to life. I went downstairs, where everyone was waiting. So many people started kissing me, I couldn't even see. The first thing I did was greet my dad and ask if my brother was still in prison. He was. That was so painful for me. Why was I released and he wasn't?

We drove home and my mom and aunt and little sisters were waiting for me in the street. We were all crying. I tried to hold myself together, but I couldn't. After that, visitors every day. What happened with you? How did you get tortured? I didn't say much, because everyone had someone in prison. I didn't want to add to their sadness.

Gradually, I decided that I needed to get active again. My mom was against this, so I had a battle with her. I told her that I needed to go out, for the sake of my brother.

A lot had changed. Because of the regime crackdown, not many people were demonstrating anymore. We put a lot of effort into trying to get them moving again. We'd throw leaflets and then run away. We'd launch balloons. We'd post pictures of political prisoners around town, writing that this person was arrested because he asked for your freedom.

One day I crossed paths with security officers again. They threw me in a car and took me to the intelligence services. They kept hitting me, saying, "You were in prison and then went back to protesting? Didn't we teach you a lesson?"

All the old memories started flooding back. The first time I was arrested, I had no idea what was going to happen. The second time was harder, because I knew what awaited me.

The beatings didn't stop for four days. And then, suddenly, an officer said, "That's it, you can leave." He sent me home. I couldn't believe it.

A few days later, I saw security cars outside my house. A friend with contacts found out that they were waiting for friends to visit me so they could get them, too. If they didn't manage to get them, they'd come back to arrest me again.

They were using me like bait: a worm to attract fish. I messaged my friends that they should stay away. And then I left for Lebanon. I just paid a bribe at the border and went right through.

## Billal, doctor (Harasta)

We were underground and couldn't see a thing. We knew it was morning when the guards switched shifts. Otherwise, we had no idea if it was night or day.

There were eighty people in our cell. Without nutrition, we all became like skeletons. People were always sick and everyone had eye infections. As a doctor, I'd try to take care of them, but I couldn't help much. I'd just tell everyone, "When it's your time to go to the bathroom, try to splash your eyes with water."

My cellmates respected me, so they let me stay near the small gate. There I could breathe a little and also see light from the corridor. Our cell was near the women's cell, and sometimes they'd come for a specific girl, calling out her name and the name of her town. We knew that they were raping her, because they always took her during the shift of a particular officer. From the small window I could see that she was about sixteen years old, and looked sick and miserable. She wore a headscarf, but they would rip it off.

There was one guy in our cell named Yousef. He cried a lot, but wouldn't say why. After three or four months, he finally told us his story. He worked as a driver for the Damascus Municipality. In the evenings, they'd take him to dig holes near the airport. Then a car would arrive filled with dead bodies. Yousef's job was to help push them into the hole and bury them. They'd throw their ID cards in the hole so no one could know what happened to them. They simply disappeared.

Once Yousef was pushing a girl's body into the hole when she moved. He realized that she was still alive, and left her to the side. The officer came and told him, "Throw her in or I'll throw you in her place." There was nothing Yousef could do, so he pushed the girl in the hole and covered her in dirt. After that he had nightmares and tried to run away. He became a wanted person, and was eventually arrested at a checkpoint and thrown in prison.

Yousef was in our cell for some time, but then one day they came and took him away. To where, I never knew.

## Omar, playwright (Damascus)

I was forty-five days old when my dad was imprisoned, and ten when he got out. Our relationship was always a struggle. As a kid, I didn't understand how prison had destroyed him, psychologically.

Then I got arrested. Prison was hell in every sense of the word. Horror, what horror. If there's anything ugly in this life, it is that security branch where I was imprisoned.

It was really hot, so we'd wear only underwear. There were so many people crowded in the cell. You'd sleep and wouldn't know who was sleeping on top of you or who was sleeping on top of him. You didn't know where your body ended and someone else's began.

At least once a day I had to carry a dead body. We new prisoners still had meat on our bones. They'd look at us and say, "You, you, and you, come here." We'd go down to the bathrooms, where corpses would be lying on their stomachs, with their faces in the basin of the squat toilet. The number of their dormitory and their files were written on their bodies. It was our job to carry the corpses and put them in a vehicle. Sometimes twelve bodies, sometimes thirteen. I once carried four myself.

There are things that you just can't communicate in words. Like the smell. Or the yellow color of the skin. The

torture, the killing, the children—there were so many children. There was this sixteen-year-old whose back was broken on the "German Chair."* There was a thirteen-year-old
named Mohammed. Once, the guard grabbed him by his
waist and pounded his head on the door. He came back to
the cell crying and lay on my stomach and started calling
me "Mama." He thought I was his mother.

The two things you feel most inside prison is despair
and hopelessness. Despair because, all of a sudden, you're
cut off from everything. You feel like an animal; no longer human. Hopelessness because you can't understand
anything. You can't do anything. You can only let things
happen to you. Hopelessness is seeing someone come
from interrogation covered in blood. Hopelessness is seeing someone else who has been there for eight months and
hasn't been asked a single question and is just begging to
be convicted and executed already. Hopelessness is waking up in the middle of the night and hearing somebody
breathing his last breaths. You bang on the door and shout
that there's somebody dying in here and they tell you,

---

* A torture method in which a detainee's arms and legs are
strapped to a chair, the back of which is pulled to the ground, caus-
ing acute pain and sometimes permanent damage to the spine.

"Leave him. Tomorrow we'll take him down to the toilets." And you can't find anywhere to sleep except on this dead person's knees.

Sometime after I was released, I was talking with my dad. I asked him how he was able to become normal again after having been in prison so long.

He looked at me and said, "Who told you that I ever became normal?"

# Fouad, surgeon (Aleppo)

My wife's brother was arrested in 1982. He had joined a leftist political party and was caught reading the party newspaper. He was the eldest son, and studying to be a doctor. The whole family had been so proud of him. He was finally released in 1997. For his father, it was like a present from God.

In prison he'd learned English and French. When he got out he became a professional translator. Given what had happened to him, his youngest son wanted to avoid anything related to politics. Instead, he worked with his dad in the translation company. He was twenty-six or so and lived in a building on the second floor. His sister lived on the first floor with her husband and son, who was a college student.

In August 2012, officers from Air Force Intelligence knocked on the door of the sister's house. Her son opened the door. Without a word they pulled him outside and put him in a car. Then a group of officers went around the house, opening drawers, and taking mobile phones. They asked the woman where her brother was, and she said that he lived on the floor above them.

Some officers went there. The commander stayed, and

even sat down and starting drinking with her husband and his friend, who were there watching TV. Then they took him and his friend away. They ended up taking four men. They took the men's cars, saying, "It's night and they'll spend a few hours with us. After that, they can come back home on their own."

The four men haven't been seen since. They've disappeared. We have no idea what happened to them. We tried. We paid money. We tried . . .

My father-in-law is eighty. He is a remnant of a person. My sister-in-law refuses to leave Damascus. We encouraged her to seek asylum elsewhere, but she said no. She will stay and wait for her husband, her brother, and her son.

# Part V

# MILITARIZATION

## Captain, FSA fighter (Aleppo)

When demonstrations began, the security forces would come. We'd throw rocks at them, and they'd use tear gas against us. Then they started opening fire on us. We agreed that if they were going to shoot bullets, then we needed weapons, too. The situation was one of murder, and we had to attack those who attacked us.

We were only chanting in the streets. We could have chanted for the rest of our lives without anyone even paying attention to us. But when the regime started attacking us, a lot of people who were on the sidelines started to join and protest, too. Because of the blood. Blood is what moves people. Blood is the force of the revolution.

# Aziza, school principal (Hama)

The American and French ambassadors attended the 500,000-person demonstration in Hama. They were welcomed with enormous enthusiasm. Women and children and men took to the streets and kids carried olive branches and flowers. You can't imagine the amount of joy and hope. People thought that Western countries supported them.

My husband is from Homs and became a protest leader there. Violence was becoming intense in Homs, but they still had chants like "One, one, one! The Syrian people are one!" When the situation worsened, they chanted, "O Alawites, we're your family. The house of Assad does not benefit you." In Rastan, a town in the Homs countryside, most residents are religious Sunni Muslims. My husband went there to express condolences after a lot of people were killed. He told them, "They want to split us along religious lines. But religion is for God and the nation is for all." The people of Rastan repeated after him, "Religion is for God and the nation is for all!"

The more people tried to address the issue of sectarianism, the more violent the regime became. It sent shabeeha to do house raids. They'd enter and kidnap young women in front of their parents.

The men said that they needed weapons to defend themselves. I urged against this. I said, "They're trying to force you into killing, which is what they want." I asked them, "Do you have tanks or planes? They have an army created to fight Israel. You don't stand a chance."

They'd say, "We have been patient. We've endured and endured, but they have ripped our women from our hands. How can we sit by and do nothing?"

## Abu Samir, defected officer (Douma)

I was in Douma and saw a massacre from my window. There was a demonstration and, toward the end, the regime started shooting. There are merciful ways to kill. But this was different. Unarmed people were killed in a horrific way. They smashed someone's head on the ground. They dragged corpses in the street.

The same day, I spoke with my brother-in-law and told him that I needed a few strong men. We formed an armed group of seven and I was the eighth. Three of us had Kalashnikovs. The rest had hunting rifles. We asked for money here and there, and went to smuggling areas in Syria and Lebanon to buy arms and ammunition.

We started working at night. We'd go to checkpoints and military installations, carry out an operation, and come back. A lot of friends and relatives objected on the grounds that this would bring bloody consequences. I told them this is a bloody regime. It is going to slaughter us. So either we defend ourselves and our families or . . .

# Abed, defected officer (Palmyra)

We were four officers in the Syrian army, with the credentials to prove to it. We had freedom of movement in all of Syria and used it to help the demonstrators. We distributed humanitarian aid and food and medical supplies to areas that needed it.

Our car did not get searched. When I'd arrive at a military site or checkpoint, I'd get out my ID. The soldier would salute. "My respects, sir, please proceed!" As an officer in the Syrian army, you're above everyone. Stand in line? Forget it! That's how the regime worked in Syria. We understood this.

The revolution started in March. Civilians and rebels started using arms in August. I told them from the beginning that this regime would not go except with force of arms. Like it or not, you have to use weapons. Every day there were peaceful demonstrations and five or six or ten people would die . . . We weren't going to get anywhere. And if you wanted to wait for world public opinion to support us, forget it. We needed to forget that myth.

By the end of 2011, things started tightening around us. It was as if the other officers suspected us. The regime's maneuvers kept failing, so they had the feeling that people were helping the insurgents from the inside.

At that time, my assignment was away from the base. One day the commanding officers sent a young lieutenant to tell me to report back to their offices. I was surprised. I asked him why they didn't communicate with me directly. He said he didn't know.

I didn't like the situation. I asked the lieutenant if I could use his mobile, saying that the minutes on mine had expired. This was just a pretext; I wanted to use his phone to call the commander and see what he would say. As soon as I put my hand on the phone a text message arrived. It was from the same commander who had sent for me. I opened it and read, "Keep your eyes on Abed, we're coming to get him."

I replied, "Received," and then erased the message. I returned the phone and thanked him. Then I took my bag and got out of there as fast as I could. The next month, I left the country.

# Ashraf, artist (Qamishli)

If international powers had intervened at the beginning, it wouldn't have reached this point. Or at least if a no fly-zone had been enforced, things wouldn't have gotten so bad.

The problem is not that the world did nothing. It's that they told us, "Rise up! We are with you. Revolt!" [Turkish president Recep Tayyip] Erdoğan declared that the bombing of Homs was a red line, and President Obama said that chemical weapons were a red line. People were encouraged to stand by the revolution because they thought they had international supporters. And when the regime crossed these lines and there was no implementation of these threats, the population was left in a state of desperation. It understood that it could count only on itself.

# Abdul Rahman, engineer (Hama)

The demonstration in Hama was like paradise. The sound of the voices was like an earthquake. Half a million free men and free women, together.

After that, the security forces ran away. We liberated Hama with numbers, not weapons. Each neighborhood made its own checkpoints to block regime forces from re-entering. We knew it was a matter of time before the army invaded, and we wanted to protect ourselves. I became a Molotov cocktail expert. We collected donations and my cousin and others smuggled weapons from north Lebanon. We got lists of weapons we could buy: An AK-47 cost 150,000 Syrian pounds. A PKC machine gun cost 175,000. A box of PKC bullets cost 15,000. We also bought ammunition from members of the regime security forces. We had spies inside the police so we kept up to date on lists of people wanted by the regime.

I had been saving money to marry my fiancé, so I was caught in a struggle between my personal life and my desire to get a gun to protect my people. That was something I'd always dreamt of, to be honest. But there was a list of guys waiting to obtain a weapon, and I was not at the top. I hadn't done military service like the others, so I lacked experience with how to handle arms.

On July 31, the regime started to shell the city at 6:30 in the morning. You could smell gunfire and hear the shudders. People started to block the streets with rocks. In our neighborhood we had nothing but two AK-47s and three pistols. One person had a grenade—where he got it, I don't know. We started filling Molotov cocktails, and distributing them to the other checkpoints. We thought that we were strong enough to stop anything.

The sounds of engines came closer and closer, and then suddenly, *boom!* They shelled us. We were twelve people at our checkpoint; seven were killed, and five, including me, slipped away with injuries. Our neighborhood was weak and our defenses broke down. We hadn't done a thing. We didn't even start.

The first day of the siege Hama showed some resistance. The second day there was no resistance. Regime forces invaded, killed 309 people, and then withdrew again. The third morning there was hard shelling. I woke up and found my sister crying and my mother reciting her will. They begged to flee Hama. I had refused up until then, but finally agreed. Everyone was running from Hama although nobody knew where.

We made it to Damascus, where I waited fifteen days. When I returned to Hama, I found it a completely changed place. Everywhere there were army checkpoints, photos of

Bashar al-Assad, and big machine guns. I walked around and saw writing on the walls, like: "There is no God but Bashar," and "Assad, or we'll burn down the country."

People continued to try to carry out some small acts of resistance, like a commercial strike, just to show the military that we were still there. It was around that time that the idea of the Free Syrian Army (FSA) emerged. I was still waiting for my turn to get a weapon when my cousin learned that I was on the wanted list. For the next month, I slept in a different bed every night so I wouldn't get caught and arrested.

We kept waiting for some good news from other cities—victories or assistance that would alleviate the pressure on Hama. My cousin told me, "You're wanted on the provincial level, but not yet at the level of all of Syria. There's still time. If you're going to flee, you should do it now."

All of my dreams were in the revolution. I was not a coward and I wanted to complete what we started. But somehow my family convinced me to leave. On September 15, I wrote slogans on the walls for the last time. I wrote, "Free Hama" and "Tomorrow will be better."

# Abdel-Halim, fighter (Homs)

I was majoring in linguistics in college, and in 2010 I started my compulsory military service. When the revolution began, I thought the regime was defending the people. In the army, they only showed us Syrian state TV channels, which were all propaganda. Then I went home to Homs and saw the destruction. When I defected, my parents reported that I was missing—kidnapped by terrorists. That way, they wouldn't be harmed because of my defection.

I joined the FSA as an accountant supervising funds and supplies. Our group grew, and when we were about 150 people, we started going out to battles. I was shot in the leg and my parents wanted to get me to Turkey for treatment, but I refused to leave. I loved what we were doing back then. We were like brothers—more than brothers, actually; it was like we were one person. Those are the memories that destroy me now.

Then the army entered Homs. They said that they wanted to inspect houses for terrorists and leave. But they came and never left. That is how the siege began.

Civilians started fleeing, but we stayed. For the first two or three months, we ate everything in the houses that residents had abandoned. Of course some families didn't flee. Our mission was to protect them and protect ourselves. When the army attacked, we'd attack back. There were battles and people died. Reinforcements came to our area through underground sewers, bringing supplies and help.

The first six months were mostly good. Then we ran out of fuel for cars. There was no electricity, except for one generator per battalion. We thought that we might stay like that for a month or two. But the situation lasted two years.

The doctors in the field hospital took care of us as much as they could, but there was no medicine. The operating room wasn't even sanitized. If someone got shot in the hand, they'd have to amputate so it wouldn't get worse. Same thing for an injured leg or foot or eye.

The real hunger began. Everyone would go out and collect leaves and plants. People who knew how to cook would boil them in water, adding spices and bouillon cubes. They did their best to make the meals seem varied and plentiful, but at the end of the day it was just grass. In the beginning we didn't feel the loss of nutrients. By the last three months of the siege, we could hardly walk. Eventually, the trees had no leaves left. We didn't know the source of the water we drank; we had the feeling it was coming from near dead bodies in the mud.

In the beginning the FSA didn't have commanders and conscripts. We were just a bunch of friends. Then dollars started flowing into the commanders' pockets. The good ones got killed or pushed aside. The bad ones became more powerful. They had heating and hidden food rations. They even cooperated with the regime army to get cigarettes.

And then there was the filming problem. At first, we filmed what we were doing to preserve a personal memory of what we were living. Then leaders started filming to get money and getting money to film. They'd go to an empty area and fire mortars to make it look like they were attacking the army. They'd send the film to external patrons, states like Turkey and Qatar, and get paid to put the footage on TV.

Eventually we started to hate everything called "leadership." We even had a protest against them. Money sent us backward. Things became like they used to be under Bashar, if not worse. Our goal had been to remove all corruption; our commanders ruined everything.

There were informants among us, too. Maybe for the regime army, maybe for the FSA leadership. We no longer knew who was with us or against us. By the end, I was just waiting for death. I'd try to calm myself by praying and reading the Quran daily. What gave me most peace was when I was able to talk on Skype with my mom and dad.

Some guys said they wanted to surrender. One went over to talk to the army and then others did the same thing. For

us, this was a huge betrayal. I would not go shake hands
with the people who killed our brothers and sisters. Besides, when I defected, my family told them that I'd gone
missing. If the army realized that I was actually a fighter
under siege for two years, they'd kill them.

Some guys rigged a car to send it over to the army, like a
suicide mission. But it exploded in our territory first. Many
people died, including good friends. I went to the hospital
to see them one last time. In one corner there was a mix of
body parts from five different people. They couldn't identify them, so they buried them all together.

One thing after another was closing in on us. I felt darkness approaching. Then a deal was proposed to evacuate us
from the Homs old city to the countryside. Some fighters
were opposed. They said they hadn't lost everything just to
leave their land. The majority was in favor, just to put an
end to our misery. We could barely move our bodies by that
point. In the end, the battalion leader accepted and we all
had to go along with his decision. The bigwigs called the
shots and we were just pawns.

May 24, 2014, was the evacuation. The Homs governor
and the army were present. Snipers were on the roofs and
cameramen were filming. When we came out, they saw
how frail we were and were shocked. It was as if they were

thinking, "*These* are the guys we were too afraid to go in and attack?"

Our bodies were weak, but we were filled with dignity. We had defended Homs to the best of our abilities. I hoped that I'd put something forth for God and for my parents. I said goodbye to everything. I lived two years in this area and it became a part of me, like my hands or my eyes. I looked at Homs and thought, "I'm not going to see her again." And it's true, I'm not. She's gone now.

## Abu Firas, fighter (rural Idlib)

For every action there is a reaction. When the regime is killing in this way, people become what we call jihadists and you call terrorists. I swear to God that I have nothing but respect for you regardless of your ethnicity, religion, or nationality. But when my sister is arrested and they rape her, I have no problem entering any place in the world with a car strapped with explosives. Because no country in the world is paying attention to me. Not a single one is doing anything to protect any fraction of the rights that I should have as a human being living on earth.

I'm not saying that the conscience of the international community is asleep. I'm saying that conscience doesn't exist at all.

## Khalil, defected officer (Deir ez-Zor)

I was a colonel serving in the Fourth Brigade and we were sent to put down demonstrations in Daraya and Muadami-yah. The commanders told us that we were fighting armed gangs. I knew this was false, but these were military orders and you don't debate military orders.

For the first two weeks, we used batons, and Air Force Intelligence officers and snipers would shoot from behind us. By the third week, they gave us orders to open fire at demonstrators' legs. If they approached within two hundred meters, we were supposed to shoot to kill.

The first time I saw a demonstration was like ecstasy. Inside, I was thrilled. But I also witnessed, with my own eyes, how the army was full of rage and resentment. I remember going to raid the house of someone accused of funding demonstrations. The officers hit the man. When his wife tried to intervene, they hit her, too. Then they hit their little girl so hard that she was thrown against the wall.

My heart was with the people from the beginning, but if the army knew you were going to defect, they'd kill you. Before I could defect, I needed to ensure the safety of my wife and children. Once I was able to do that, I fabricated a scenario to make it seem like I'd been kidnapped, and then I disappeared. For a while, it wasn't clear to the army if I'd been captured or actually defected. During that time, they arrested my father and brother. They released my dad after a few days, but held my brother longer.

Then the regime came to my house in Damascus. They stole what they could and burned the rest. They did the same thing to my family home in Deir ez-Zor. I'm not crying over the loss of the houses. The point is that I have nowhere to go back to.

They offered a reward to anyone who could provide information on my whereabouts and a bigger one for anyone who killed me. I moved around from place to place at night. At the same time, I began working with the FSA.

Then the Nusra Front emerged. In June 2012, I went to talk to them. I saw them as a threat to our own security. They were raising al-Qaeda's Black Flag. I said, "This is a popular revolution, why don't you use the revolution's flag?"

They said, "That's the flag of the infidels. We're raising the flag of the Prophet."

I said, "Okay, the Prophet is in our hearts. But raising this flag is going to cause us a lot of problems. Why do you want to do this now?"

They said, "We've been rebelling against the regime since before the revolution began, but we were in prison."

I asked, "Which prison?"

They said, "Sadnaya. We were released in April."

I asked them, "What were your charges?"

They said, "Antiregime activity."

That's when it became clear to me. The regime had allowed these people to go to Iraq to fight the Americans. Then they came back to Syria, and the regime put them in prison. And now the regime was using them for leverage.

I said, "Bashar let you go so he could say that he is fighting terrorism."

They replied, "God willed that this should be done and he made Bashar take that decision."

We each went forward with our work separately. We in the FSA would attack a regime position, force the regime to withdraw, and move on to the next regime position. Meanwhile, Nusra would come along behind us and take control of the point we'd just liberated. We were focused on fighting the regime while Nusra was looking to occupy territory.

Most of Nusra's fighters were foreigners—Saudis, Qataris, Tunisians . . . The FSA had more men, but received little aid. We could afford to give fighters only a one-time payment. Nusra gave its fighters monthly salaries and top-quality weapons. Nusra distributed bread to people to try to win their support. People took it because they were hungry, but the first opportunity they had to go out and protest against Nusra, they did.

Then ISIS emerged. Abu Mohammed al-Jolani was responsible for Nusra, which was like a faction of al-Qaeda. Abu Bakr al-Baghdadi made ISIS, and part of the movement left with him. ISIS also paid people to join its ranks. It offered money, weapons, and ammunition.

Raqqa became the ISIS headquarters. There was no battle; the regime just handed it to them and left. ISIS imprisoned hundreds of FSA fighters and civilians. Once, we were transporting ammunition supplies from the FSA Supreme Military Council in Turkey to Deir ez-Zor and had to pass through Raqqa. ISIS arrested the driver and seized the ammunition. We were in dire need of that ammunition. Fighters called me and said, "Tell us if we're getting more supplies or not. Because if not, we'd be better off just surrendering to ISIS."

We don't accept ISIS. We're against Assad because he's a dictator. We won't accept another dictator to take his place. What gives them the right to say that something is blasphemy? ISIS killed a German doctor working in a field hospital, saying he was an infidel. This man had come from abroad to treat injured people. If that's infidel, let us all be infidels like him.

## Husayn, playwright (Aleppo)

The FSA launched its attack on Aleppo, and the city entered the revolution's military stage. The city became divided between regime areas and liberated areas. The FSA took over the poorer neighborhoods—more than half the city. People were worried about survival. As revolutionary activists, the most important thing we could do was offer people an alternative to the regime. We had to provide food, shelter, and services. We had to create a new system.

Building on that idea, we held elections for local councils to represent Aleppo city and all of Aleppo province. The elections were the first of its kind in Syria. It was one of the most important experiences of my life. I invested all of my political experience into it, because I believed that we had to make it work. We wanted to build real institutions that could develop the state.

The main competition was between us revolutionaries and the Muslim Brotherhood, which was very organized and had a lot of money. We had only words. We walked around neighborhoods all day long, talking about our goals and principles. People still appreciated us back then. Later, money and relief aid started flowing in, and they stopped caring. Now if I went and talked to them about the revolution's values, they'd kick me out.

At that time, there were thousands of abandoned homes in Aleppo. The armed battalions simply took over empty houses. We activists insisted on getting permission from the rightful owners. A man from Aleppo who was working in Saudi Arabia donated his house for our use, and it became like a beehive of activity. More than thirty of us slept on foam mattresses. Everyone took turns cleaning and cooking. One guy was rich, so he'd buy kebab. Others were poor, and could only afford to make eggs.

Whenever people went to pray, I'd keep doing whatever I was doing. No one ever pressured me to join. They knew that I'm secular, but treated me with respect, as an old man who left his family to help the revolution. One activist friend became a Salafist and grew a long beard. He lived in a distant neighborhood and it was dangerous to walk at night, because there was no electricity and no lights. He told the others that if he couldn't make meetings, he gave me permission to vote on his behalf. There wasn't religious extremism at the beginning. It took time and effort to get people to become extremists. I think the impetus was from outside the country, and money and weapons were the main drivers.

We created the first movement against Islamization after Islamic groups killed a fourteen-year-old who used to sell coffee on the street. Three Islamists—an Egyptian, a Tunisian, and a Syrian—wanted to take coffee and pay the boy later. He told them, "Even if the Prophet Mohammed came I wouldn't give it to him on credit." The Islamists considered that blasphemy and killed the boy.

We called our movement "Enough is Enough." We started organizing small civic campaigns. One, called "Don't be part of the chaos," urged people not to drive cars without license plates. Another, called "I want my school," asked battalions to return schools that they had seized as military centers.

It was around that time that ISIS arrived in Aleppo. They started kidnapping journalists and activists, including Abu Mariam, who was a famous protest leader. There were few of us left by then, but we organized a sit-in in front of the ISIS headquarters demanding Abu Mariam's release. We felt safe, relatively speaking, because ISIS wasn't as powerful then as it is now. But an ISIS car followed us home and, along the way, blocked our taxi in the street. That was a way of sending the message that they were watching us.

After that, we began working in secret. I moved into another neighborhood run by a warlord known to be a violent killer. He didn't allow ISIS in and promised to protect anyone living under his control. I faced a dilemma. I didn't want to ally with any armed group. But I was accepting protection from a violent killer, so people would consider me to be on his side.

That was the point when I felt that I had become useless. I decided to leave Syria. I no longer had a purpose for staying.

## Kinda, activist (Suwayda)

By 2012, the FSA, Nusra Front, and other groups had emerged. There were ugly incidents. A cease-fire was declared, but no one was respecting it, of course.

My sister and I met with a few friends to figure out what we could do. We came up with the most wonderful idea. Four of us would wear bridal dresses. It's a beautiful sight, a white dress with a veil. Our message was to both sides: Enough! End the killing.

Our parents were supportive. They stood by our side even though other relatives refused to talk to us. They were pro-regime, like most Druze. We started making the dresses. We got fabric and a sewing machine and asked a seamstress for help. I told myself that if I died wearing that white dress in protest, I would die on Syrian land with pride. The rest of the world would know that we're not terrorists.

The preparations took about twenty-five days. We had a party the day before we went out. We decorated with jasmine flowers, as people do for weddings in Damascus. We prepared signs. One read, "I'm 100 percent Syrian." Another read, "Syria is for all of us." The third sign read, "Civil society calls to end all military operations on Syrian land."

The next day we went down to Midhat Basha market.

We had to pass through checkpoints to get there, so we wore black abayas over the wedding dresses. Friends met us in the market; they dispersed into the crowd with the plan to come together once the protest began.

One of the girls counted. One, two, three, and we took off our black abayas. The white dresses appeared and we put on the veils. We raised the signs and stood there for about seven minutes. People were shocked. We were four brides in the middle of the market, and we brought it to a standstill. It was a wonderful scene, by far the most beautiful day of my life.

Then we started walking. Store owners left their stores and came to watch us. Everyone was filming with their cell phones, but was silent. I wanted to move them, so I said, "Why aren't you ululating for Syria's brides?" I ululated, and the crowd went crazy ululating and clapping for us. I remember there was an elderly man who began to cry. We did not hear a single curse or insult. People were saying, "God bless you. You are the heroes of Syria."

A security force member came, a gun in his hand. He told me, "Take that sign down and don't cause problems." I raised my sign even higher. We became more determined. You felt like you were facing an executioner: It's either you or him.

The whole protest lasted about half an hour before a full

security detail arrived on the scene and detained us. They threatened us and cursed our mothers and brothers. They kept demanding, "Who are you working for? Who's behind you?" Then they took us to the branch office. We heard them say among themselves, "Why did those filthy whores go out? Were they looking for someone to ride them? Why don't we take them down to the jihadists? One hundred jihadists would take each bride." It was terrifying psychological torture. Your mind fills with questions. Will they really do that?

They had us wait in the corridor. You see bloodstains on the wall and ask yourself, "Whose blood is that?" You see older men, barefoot and kneeling on the floor. You wonder how long they've been like that. You see young men with their heads covered. They beat them as they pleased. We saw the guys cuffed and hanging from rods, metal digging into their flesh. I remember one guy telling the officer, "Father, please, I kiss your hand. Please take me down, just give me thirty seconds to use the bathroom." The officer told him, "No. And if you do it on yourself, I'll make you drink it."

After a while they took us away for interrogation, one by one. Interrogation lasted from three o'clock in the afternoon until eight the next morning. Then they took us down to the cell. Every day we'd hear the shots of field executions.

We got sick and got lice. In the cell, there was one person with epilepsy, three people with asthma, one person with ovarian cancer. We were a tiny room with twenty-five diseases. For fifteen days, my sister was on the verge of death. I started beating down the door. I screamed at the guard, "I don't need my sister. She will die for the sake of Syria, but you will be held accountable." They were afraid because we were from a religious minority. The next day, the doctor came.

We stayed in prison for two months, and then were released on a prisoners exchange. After I got out, I went back to Midhat Basha market and asked the shop owners about the brides incident. One said, "Yes, I remember. They arrested them."

I told him that I was one of the brides. He hugged me and started crying. He said, "Do you know what happened the next day here?" He told me that there was an old man who used to sell children's toys, displayed on a table. The day after our protest he cleared everything off his table and put up only four dolls dressed as brides. Just four brides.

# Part VI

# LIVING WAR

## Abu Firas, fighter (rural Idlib)

It's been so long since I heard that someone died from natural causes.

In the beginning, one or two people would get killed. Then twenty. Then fifty. Then it became normal. If we lost fifty people, we thought, "Thank God, it's only fifty!"

I can't sleep without the sounds of bombs or bullets. It's like something's missing. Last year, they shelled the market on the holiday at the end of Ramadan. People left the market. Half an hour later, everyone returned and went back to buying and selling.

# Rana, mother (Aleppo)

It was a nightmare in every meaning of the word. Or like a horror movie come true. The feeling of terror is indescribable. I got physically ill from the stress and pressure. Even now, I have all sorts of digestive problems.

We were bombed in the winter and all the windows broke. My son's lips would turn blue from the cold. Finally we had to flee the house with only the clothes that we were wearing. We spent eight months living in different places. Sometimes we found places to rent and sometimes we didn't. It was like a vacation, but with bombing. Now even my three-year-old can tell the difference between different missiles and rockets.

My family lives in the countryside. I didn't see them for six months. Then when I finally went to visit, they bombed those areas, too. The adults and ten kids slept in the entryway, but we didn't actually sleep the whole night. The bombs would explode and the door would dance, shaking from the impact. After a bombing, the sky would become brown from all the dust and dirt thrown up into the air.

We went back home but the bombing continued. I'd call my mom and ask, "Have they bombed you over there, or not yet?"

## Amin, physical therapist (Aleppo)

There were parts of Syria where my experience as a physical therapist was needed, like in the camps for the internally displaced. So I found myself working in such a camp. I had the idea that I was going to help people. But I realized that, three years after the start of the revolution, people didn't care anymore. We'd approach a patient saying, "We want to treat you so you can walk again." He'd say, "I'm finished. I just want to die." Or there would be kids, and we'd tell them, "You need to get an education. You need to . . ." And the children would say, "I don't want to be dragged around in a wheelchair anymore. The other boys make fun of me." There was one child from the camp with polio. He used to come and say to me, "When I was a little kid . . ." And he was only ten years old.

Every time someone dies we say we need to continue, we need to continue. But continue what? We're coming to a dead end. I saw so many of my friends die. Friends die in the revolution and friends in my army unit when I was still doing my compulsory service. They were so young. Once I was talking to this guy and his only dream was to talk to his mother again. We had no means of communication then, and he died before he could speak to her or anyone else.

Another time, one of the other guys called his girlfriend and said, "Sweetheart, I'm out of minutes on my phone. I'll call you back on Amin's phone." After a while she called me asking about him, and I told her that he'd been killed. She cried and my friends said, "Why did you tell her that?" I said, "Because that's what happened. It's normal. He died."

This is when we lost our humanity. I'd open my phone and look at my contacts and only one or two were still alive. They told us, "If someone dies, don't delete his number. Just change his name to 'Martyr.'" That way, if you got a text from that number, you knew that someone else had gotten hold of the phone and might be using it to entrap you.

So I'd open my contact list and it was all *Martyr, Martyr, Martyr . . .*

## Jalal, photographer (Aleppo)

In the beginning, we filmed protests on our phones. Later we were able to bring in more advanced cameras and taught ourselves how to use them. Foreign journalists started coming. I'd go out with them as a fixer and watch how they worked with photos. By 2013, I was working with news agencies as a photographer myself.

Some people have a good instinct for battle photos or for photos of everyday civilian life. I love photos of hope; hope in the midst of death. For example, I took several photos of a vendor with a cart of oranges. Behind him, the building is completely collapsed. It's night. The oranges are hit by a glimmer of light, and you see that they're wiped clean. For sure, this man has witnessed many people die. But in spite of everything, he's standing there, selling this delicious fruit. You see this image and think, "This is life."

At the same time, whatever comes out of these people is understandable, as far as I'm concerned. The regime has turned us into monsters so it can justify killing us by saying that it's fighting monsters. Syrian society has been shattered, because families have been shattered. Bring any family together today and you'll find four or five empty chairs.

I once photographed a barrel bomb that killed three kids. I was photographing the father as he sobbed. He kept saying, "I left them for one hour to look for a safer place to take them. I came back and they were gone." I have four kids, and the whole purpose of my future is to guarantee their future. So I imagine this man who loses his kids—the thing that defines his future. I completely understand if he turns into a monster.

But even a monster has hope. He hopes that someday he'll go back to being a normal human being.

## Kareem, doctor (Homs)

The operating room was in use around the clock. For each surgery, we took an X-ray. It's just a fraction of a second, but we took so many that we calculated that we were exposed to about twenty minutes of radiation a week. Once we received a young man who had been shot by a sniper and needed surgery by a vascular specialist. None were able to reach the hospital due to the siege, so one gave us instructions over the phone, and we carried out the surgery as he directed.

One Sunday I spent the night at the hospital and woke up to intense shooting. Regime forces were shelling Baba Amr and occupying the whole neighborhood. Seven of us fled to the basement. We hid and listened to the tanks get closer.

We heard a group storm the hospital. They were shooting bullets and shattering glass. We thought we were done for. The regime viewed doctors as partners with the rebels. As far as it was concerned, if you treated the brother of someone who participated in a demonstration, then you both deserved to be punished.

We waited like sheep to be slaughtered. And then we had an idea. One of us was brave enough to shout, "Where are you? We're down here!" We tried to show that we were only civilians who had nothing to do with the fighting. They called us up and we saw them: eight people, armed to the teeth. The leader was a shabeeh wearing a belt filled with knives. He spoke with an Alawite accent. The rest were just kids, conscripts in the army who didn't know what they were doing or why.

The shabeeh commanded us down to the basement again. We thought that he would drop a grenade and kill us, but suddenly they left and the hospital became calm again. Half an hour later, another group came, also breaking things and opening fire. We tried the same trick; it worked, and again they ordered us to stay in the basement.

We waited for them to come down and kill us. It didn't happen. Instead, a terrible burning smell descended into the basement. I felt like I was going to choke. I went upstairs and saw that they'd broken into the administration office. They'd stolen all the money there, which must have made them forget about us. And then they burned the place to hide the crime.

We managed to extinguish the fire, but the smoke made it impossible to breathe. A tank was parked at the main gate of the hospital; if we exited from the front, we'd be arrested or killed. The only option was to go out the back, climb over the wall behind the hospital, and seek refuge in the residential building on the other side. So that's what we did.

One nurse weighed over two hundred pounds, but sheer fear carried her over, too. It turned out that the army had just searched that building. If we'd climbed ten minutes earlier, we would have been caught.

We stayed with the neighbors for seven days, eating rice and stale bread, and sitting in the dark without electricity. Two patients remained in the hospital. One was in intensive care, hooked up to a ventilator. A nurse and the hospital guard stayed with her until there was no oxygen left. When the patient died, they jumped over the wall and joined us.

The second patient had been shot in the frontal lobe. He was there with his son, who was maybe eleven years old. The boy would leave at night, knock on doors asking for help, and then go back to his dad. On the third day, the army entered the hospital and killed them both. We saw them take the corpses away.

The attack on Baba Amr was the first time the army used surface-to-surface missiles, rocket launchers, and airplanes. The international community said nothing, so the regime continued using them after that. Eventually, they announced an agreement that allowed civilians to go out. I didn't know it at the time, but I was in a shock that lasted about fifteen days. I kept thinking, "What happened? How did I survive? Why am I not dead?"

I returned to my house and found that the army had been staying there. A stray cat was inside and the house was flooded with water and diesel. Most of the furniture was stolen and whatever was left was ruined. All of the house's privacy was violated. My private things, my wife's private things . . . they wrote on the wall, "This is freedom."

Imagine that you find your own neighborhood looking like Hiroshima. Destruction. Buildings knocked to the ground. A strange calm . . . as if you're in a theater. Silence. Only the tweet of sparrows.

## Hiba, former student (Qalamoun)

I was studying pharmacy in Damascus. Then things got agitated in our area. The checkpoints made it too difficult to reach campus. I took leave for the semester and my family went back home to Qalamoun.

My dad was on the board of directors for a charitable organization, and I started working with them to help people who had fled from other parts of Syria. We thought of them as our guests. We did other projects, too. Kids were getting really bored stuck inside all the time, so we worked with them to put on a show with music and dancing.

Qalamoun is near the border with Lebanon, so there were conflicts every now and then. Normally there would be shelling followed by airstrikes, and then everything would go back to normal. November 2013 was different. Airstrikes started and didn't stop for twenty-five days. The battle of Qalamoun had begun.

We hid in the basement. My dad and brother refused to stay with us. They spent the days working at the charity, where people were bringing the injured. One day, dad came home and I could tell that he was hiding something. Finally he told us; my brother had been martyred. The bullet had gone in his neck. He remained alive for a while, but no one had the means to save him. Later they tried to bring him to the cemetery to bury him, but there was too much shooting and they had to turn back.

After that, mom was in a bad psychological state. Dad urged us to go to Damascus so she could rest a bit. He refused to leave Qalamoun. It was his town and there was still work for him to do.

We left, and he stayed. Then the regime took over the area and started arresting people. They targeted board members of the charity on the suspicion that they were assisting the FSA.

One evening we called dad but his phone was off. We kept calling and calling. Fifteen days passed and we heard nothing. Then we received a text from his number saying, "I ran away." Ran away? I was suspicious. I texted back, "Call us on your wife's number." He had mom's number memorized, but not saved on his mobile.

He didn't call. We waited and waited and he didn't call . . . and that's how we knew that it wasn't him.

We asked around at different security branches. We asked and asked. We used every connection we had and paid whatever they wanted. They always made us promises like, "Next month . . ."

Months went by and at some point, a man called us. He'd just been released from prison, where he'd been with my dad. He told us, "He's lost some weight, but he's strong.

He's only worried about you." I asked if there was any way to send him a message, to tell him that I gave birth to a little girl, and my sister got married, and we're doing okay? He said that he'd try.

With time you get used to the idea that your brother has died. You say, "This is the situation for everyone in the country, not just us." This is fate. This is what God has written for us. But the feeling that my dad might be in prison, waiting for us to do something . . . I blame myself. I did everything I could do, but somehow I should have done more.

Sometimes with the daily routine, you forget a bit. But then some little thing happens and it comes back to you. Like last year, there were two big snowstorms. I'd cover myself with blankets and immediately think, "Oh God, how is dad staying warm now?"

## Osama, student (al-Qusayr)

The first time the army came into al-Qusayr, they arrested a lot of people or beat them in the streets. The second time and third time, they shot people. After that, guys started taking up guns. Al-Qusayr became really dangerous. There was shelling, like in other towns. A sniper was positioned on a tall building near the main street and shot anyone who passed. My dad had a bus and would drive people across the street so nobody got hurt. He became wanted by the regime and then they arrested him and took him away.

People started buying weapons, and the armed groups grew. I was spending all my time outside, asking a lot of questions. I was just in ninth grade, and my family was afraid for my safety. One day mom told me that we needed to go to Jordan because my grandfather was sick. We were going to visit him and then return home. But it turned out that they tricked me; we went to Jordan and never came back. I was so upset that they did this to me.

Meanwhile, Hezbollah wanted to come from Lebanon to Syria to help the regime. One way was through al-Qusayr, because it's right on the border. The FSA shot at the Hezbollah fighters, and the regime started shelling. The regime didn't care that it killed people; it just wanted to take the city so its allies could get through. Hezbollah moved in and all the people left, except for poor people who didn't have the means to leave. Forces from Hezbollah, Iran, and Russia encircled the town.

The people of al-Qusayr withstood for three months. I think it's remarkable that they held out for so long. Al-Qusayr became known worldwide. On the news, you'd hear, "Poor al-Qusayr, the town is being destroyed." People in other countries sent money, but the leaders of different FSA brigades took it for themselves. They put it in their pockets while the young guys were dying. I couldn't understand: Why did they want money so much when they could die at any moment?

The Syrian army focused on al-Qusayr and took it over. A lot of people said that was a turning point. And because it is my hometown, I felt that the revolution had failed. I lost all hope. I stopped listening to the news or following events. When al-Qusayr fell, I felt that I became a refugee.

## Rami, graduate (Yarmouk camp)

I grew up in the Yarmouk refugee camp. It's a special place, like the capital of the Palestinian diaspora. It's called a camp, but it doesn't look like a camp. It was just a well-developed district in the southern part of Damascus.

The towns surrounding Yarmouk got involved in the armed conflict, and people from those areas sought refuge in the camp. There was sort of a consensus among armed groups to keep it as a neutral zone.

Then in July 2012, the intelligence headquarters in Damascus was bombed. It killed two ministers and shook the whole security apparatus. This began a new phase in the life of Damascus. The regime took forces from the coast and deployed them to set up checkpoints inside and outside the capital.

Meanwhile, the conflict around Yarmouk kept intensifying. Armed groups pushed security forces from parts of the Damascus suburbs, but the regime encircled and besieged them. They needed supplies, and for logistical reasons, their only access was through Yarmouk. With the agreement of the regime, Palestinian factions took up arms to prevent rebel groups from entering the camp. Those groups saw Palestinian factions as defending Assad. There were clashes, and armed groups managed to get inside the camp. They roamed around, filming videos saying that they liberated the camp.

That day, all of a sudden, there was a mixed shelling of the camp. It targeted the mosque and a school. The noise and casualties were horrifying. Residents realized they'd been dragged into the middle of the conflict. There was shock, paranoia, and fear. Very early the next morning, a mass exodus of people began. The majority of the 150,000 Palestinians living in the camp took their bags and left. I was among them.

It was the end of the camp as we knew it. People called it the second Nakba.* The Nakba of Yarmouk. Only about 20,000 people remained. They were the most vulnerable.

Bombardment continued for two weeks. If you tried to leave the camp, a regime sniper would kill you. The siege developed gradually to a complete blockade. The main entrance was blocked with sandbags and concrete. It was collective punishment, like the regime was saying, "You allowed the rebels in. This is what you deserve." Armed groups in the camp started fighting each other because they had no one else to fight.

---

* The Nakba, or "Catastrophe," is the term Palestinians use to refer to the 1948 War that led to the establishment of the state of Israel and the displacement of more than half of the Palestinian Arab population as refugees.

## Um Naji, mother (Yarmouk camp)

We should have left when the blockade was partial, but we never expected it to become complete. At first, the checkpoint would close the area one day, and open the next. And then the checkpoint closed for good. Whoever was inside the camp got stuck inside and whoever was outside got stuck outside.

I lived under the siege for nine months. We had food stored at home, but time passed and we ate all of it. Armed men or regime agents raided the shops and there was nothing left for civilians. We had money, but there was nothing to buy. Instead, my husband would collect grass and leaves and we'd fry them in olive oil. Later we couldn't even find grass. My four kids lost weight. They would lie on the floor, without energy even to speak. They were starving to death in front of me, and I couldn't do anything about it.

My uncle used connections to get us out. He tried and tried until he got permissions from different intelligence services so that my kids and I could pass through the checkpoint. My husband had to stay behind. We arrived at the checkpoint and at first they refused us. We waited all day and finally they let us through.

## Yousef, former student (rural Hasakah)

I was arrested in my second year of medical school and spent five months in prison. I was home recovering when ISIS showed up.

Syria's oil is located in our areas in the eastern part of the country and ISIS recognized how valuable that is. They took over our village and then moved on to take Deir ez-Zor, which has the largest oil reserves. Regime planes backed them up. They bombed the rebels and people, not ISIS. Now ISIS has all the oil in the area. It has the weapons, the wheat, everything.

ISIS aren't aliens, like some people describe them. They're regular people. They're an organization like other organizations. There were so many men ready to fight ISIS. Women, too. We could have beaten them, but we didn't have enough weapons. No one supported us. Instead the U.S.-led Coalition started bombing. Two months ago, twenty-seven people in my village were killed while waiting in line for bread. Coalition planes killed them.

It's airstrikes that have destroyed the country. Planes do the most damage, and ISIS doesn't have planes.

# Hakem, engineer and pharmacist (Deir ez-Zor)

The FSA took control of our area in Deir ez-Zor. All the hospitals were in regime-controlled areas, so my friend turned his house into a field hospital. I'm a pharmacist and I volunteered there. Once, I helped do a surgery to remove a bullet near a young man's heart. The electricity was out so we did the whole surgery by the light of our cell phones. The doctor who performed the surgery was a veterinarian.

When the FSA and Nusra Front were in our area, people complained because of the chaos and lack of security. ISIS claimed to want to establish security and make sure no one broke the law. They entered our area with heavy arms, Hummers, and tanks. They were strong, like a real state. The FSA and Nusra Front didn't have weapons to stop them. Most of their members just ran away.

I lived under ISIS rule for a year and a half. ISIS forced us to go out and watch them cut off people's heads. It was scary for kids at the beginning, but then they got used to it. It became normal to see a dead body hanging in the main square or a body hanging from a tree without a head. They'd keep a body out in public for two or three days, and then throw it away somewhere. ISIS took control of the oil refineries and made it clear that the oil belonged to them. They forced people to pay them taxes. Many people didn't have enough money, but they had to pay or face punishment.

I was in Deir ez-Zor when the Russian planes started attacking and when the Coalition started attacking. I can bring you a list of the civilians who got killed. For some reason, I wrote down all their names.

## Talia, TV correspondent (Aleppo)

Separating the regime and liberated parts of Aleppo was what was known as the "Death Crossing." It was a street exposed to four regime snipers who shot indiscriminately. Fifteen thousand people would pass through every day. Of those, twenty would die.

I was living in the liberated part of Aleppo. My daughter needed to see an eye doctor, so we had to go to the regime-controlled area. They would shoot more intensely just before the crossing closed at four o'clock. We made it back there around 3:45. A group of us had started crossing when they opened fire. We all dropped to the ground. My daughter and I huddled together. The man next to me didn't get up. He'd been shot. I began to cry and my daughter began reciting the Quran. It took us a half hour to make it to the other side.

My husband was in Turkey at that time. I was responsible for my mom and children. We didn't have electricity. Sometimes we could tap into a line to turn on the light or TV. There was no water, so people dug wells. Everyone in the neighborhood would go down and fill up canisters of water daily. You felt like the whole neighborhood was family. We had no heat, but we'd warm ourselves by burning this fuel used in old forms of transportation. It gave off a terrible smell. My son got asthma from that fuel, as well as from the smoke from bombs and burning garbage.

I remember when they dropped a barrel bomb for the first time. The house shook and all the windows shattered. The bomb struck near my daughter's school. I left my son with the neighbors and ran to get my daughter. It felt like the longest distance of my life. Every possible scenario entered my mind: maybe I'd find her dead. Maybe I'd see her torn to pieces. Maybe she'd be covered in ash and debris. When I found her, I decided that I wouldn't let her go to school anymore. Two weeks later, her school was bombed and sixteen kids were killed.

# Marcell, activist (Aleppo)

I'd grown up middle class. When I moved into the liberated areas of Aleppo, I discovered that there were poor people in Syria. I was a woman who didn't wear a headscarf living alone in an area where no woman was without a headscarf or lives alone. People wondered, "Why is she here? Why didn't she go to Europe like everyone else?"

It was the most challenging year of my life. Moving into the liberated areas meant knowing that I was going to die. Accepting that reality changes you a lot. It affects your mentality and all of your choices. You're always asking yourself if you could kill and you're always meeting people who are asking themselves the same thing. Like mothers saying, "If they come for my child, then I will . . ."

Living under bombs, seeing bodies shattered into pieces—no one should see that much death. A barrel bomb can easily collapse a whole building like a cardboard box. You see people who have lost everything and never had much to start with. And then . . . the feelings of guilt. You'd find yourself thinking: Should we have done things differently? Should we have done nothing at all?

It was a harsh year. Especially with regard to women's issues. It wasn't like going to a demonstration for two hours. It became a whole lifestyle. It was the fight with your friends because they don't want you to go alone in the street. You consider yourself a feminist, and say, "C'mon, do you really need to accompany me to buy a kilo of potatoes?" They say, "This is a situation of war." And I say, "No, it's a revolution!"

If the armed groups called for a rebel meeting, I'd be the only woman there. Everyone was shocked, like, "When we said rebels, we didn't expect *her* to come." I would say, "We're equals. Let's talk."

ISIS emerged. At first, no one knew who they were. The first time I recognized the problem was when a Jordanian fighter gathered children in the street and said that he'd pay a dollar to every child who threw a rock at me because I wasn't wearing a headscarf and I was walking with men who weren't my brothers. Back then, there were few of them and they didn't have enough power to arrest me directly.

Not one of the kids threw a rock, but one of their parents came by our house. He said, "Don't panic, but this is what happened. Our children won't do this. But we are afraid that others might. It's not safe."

My friends and I changed houses and I went on to change houses another ten times. That became the story of my life: packing, running, packing, sometimes running without even packing.

Then another ISIS fighter stopped me on the street one day. He said, "You can't look like that here." He was from Belgium. To me it was funny. You come here and are going to tell me what to wear? He said, "This is Islamland."

I said, "No, this is Syria."

Our exchange got tense and I started to yell. FSA fighters came and said, "What do you want from our daughter?" With their intervention, the situation passed.

Later, ISIS guys stopped me a second time. The third time, they followed me in vans. By then, five or six of my friends had already been kidnapped by ISIS. They were going to kidnap me, too. If that happened, I wouldn't be brave. I'd be stupid. I thought, "Okay. Let me leave the country for a while and see what happens." So I left for Turkey, and I was crying like a baby the whole way.

WE CROSSED A BRIDGE AND IT TREMBLED

## Haneen, graduate (Daraya)

The first massacre that I lived through was during Ramadan. I was at my sister's house and it was too dangerous to go back home because of the snipers. There was a sniper near our house, and anyone on the street would be killed.

Days passed. Finally we decided to try to go back home. We took the narrow back roads so the sniper wouldn't see us. We walked close to the walls and then hurried from one wall to another. After we got home, the missiles and rockets began. We needed a safe place to hide, so we again left to find shelter underground. The sniper was still there. It was easier for the sniper to see us as a group, so we ran by his position one at a time.

We found shelter in a basement. It had little windows onto street level, so we saw when the security forces came and then tanks followed. From underground, we could hear people yelling. Somehow we got hold of someone who talked to someone who talked to someone else who said that they were capturing people they found underground.

We were terrified. We told ourselves that whatever was going to happen was going to happen, and it would be better to die above ground than below ground. So we waited until night and again ran home as fast as we could. Back home, all the food had gone bad because it was summer and there was no electricity. We ate moldy bread, because there was no alternative. We hid anything of value, like phones and jewelry and pictures. We buried things in places that the security forces wouldn't think to search.

Security forces reached our street and executed six young men. We were in a state of terror. Then the forces left to go to another neighborhood. We had no way of knowing if they'd return or when.

We didn't go out for many days. Finally, the date came for my exam at the university. I went to take it. I was so scared that the security forces would stop me along the way. I don't even know why I went to take the exam. I just knew that we needed to keep living our lives.

The second massacre was the chemical weapons attack. Things were getting bad again, and my sister was worried about her kids. She wanted to move somewhere else, so we left with her. We thought we'd stay away only two or three days.

That next day, the regime launched chemical weapons. They hit very close to our house. My uncle and cousin were killed. It was like poison that burned their bodies from the inside. No one knew it was chemical weapons at that time. They had no scars, no wounds, no signs of anything, nothing at all. They were just dead.

## Sham, relief worker (Douma)

Rockets would fall all over Douma. They might land on the street, on a building, on the market. I lived through buildings falling before my eyes. I lived through corpses. I lived through rockets that would explode children into a million pieces. Sometimes we'd clean up body parts with our own hands. There wouldn't be a whole body to pick up. Just a hand or a leg or a head.

We were a Red Crescent emergency response team, wearing uniforms and riding in an emergency vehicle. The army wasn't supposed to bother the Red Crescent. But some days they'd scare us with their guns. Some days they'd take the injured person right out of our ambulance. We couldn't dare open our mouths.

Once, soldiers detained my friend's team. They lined them against the wall, and shot my friend in the head. We followed him to the hospital and waited. When a person came and told us he was dead, I immediately fainted. Another friend carried me away and a third friend treated me. The two of them were later killed, too. I'm telling you; all my friends have been killed.

When the intelligence officers arrested my husband, Munir, for the third time I sobbed to them, "God bless you, please don't take him. I'm so tired, I can't take it anymore." The officer said, "Everything is fine. We'll keep him for only an hour."

That hour lasted a year and one month. For the first five months, I didn't know if he was alive or dead. You know that phrase, "to disappear into thin air"? It was like the Bermuda Triangle; he disappeared and that was it. Every lawyer told me, "We'll get him out." But they were just lying so I would keep paying them.

At the end of May, my mobile rang and it was an unknown number. I was in such a terrible state of mind that I had my brother pick up the phone. I couldn't bring myself to talk to anyone. Then I heard my brother mention Munir's name. I nearly lost my mind and grabbed the phone. Munir had been transferred to a different prison branch and managed to call me.

That August was the chemical weapons attack. People will tell you that this was their version of Doomsday. In the streets you saw people frozen in their cars, suffocated to death. My colleagues told me this was the first time they picked up corpses and there was no blood. I got news that the gas had spread to the prison. I was so scared for Munir that I thought I would die. It turned out that the stench of the gas did reach them and the prisoners started coughing. They didn't know what was happening.

Obama made his announcement about the red line. People celebrated, because they thought this would finally be the end of the regime. We thought, "At last, he'll be ousted!" We got so excited—only to be disappointed again.

Meanwhile, someone connected to the regime told me that if I paid enough, he'd get Munir out of prison. The catch was that we'd have to leave the country immediately. So Munir was released. We stayed in Syria for another month and a half and then left.

Everything we've experienced has killed us. We check the news every second. This person is still alive; this person was killed. Believe me, if the world had helped us from the beginning, we never would have reached this point. Some think that we're religious fundamentalists. But nobody forces me to fast during Ramadan. Here I am smoking a cigarette. Munir is fasting, but in the morning he wakes up and makes me coffee. I swear, in Syria nobody used to ask whether you're Muslim or Christian. We had no idea what religion our friends were.

But none of that matters anymore. If I died this second, I wouldn't care. Because I've reached a point in my life where I hate everything. I am disgusted by humanity.

We're basically the living dead. Sometimes I joke to Munir that someone should gather all of us Syrians in one place and kill us so we can be done with this whole thing already. Then we'll all go to heaven and leave Bashar al-Assad to rule over an empty country.

# Part VII

# FLIGHT

## Talia, TV correspondent (Aleppo)

The night before I left was the longest night of my life. I was alone with the kids, and the planes were in the sky all night. The sound of planes is scarier than the sound of barrel bombs, because you hear them and wonder when the bombs will drop. The waiting is harder than the actual attack.

I didn't know if we'd leave the next day, or if this would be the night that we died. I had seen children torn in pieces before, but I wasn't strong enough to see my own kids in that state. I needed to get them to safety.

The kids woke up and I got them dressed. I got two pieces of paper and wrote our names and phone numbers and put them in their pockets. That way, if someone got killed, people would know their identities.

I waited for the driver outside. I kissed the walls on the street, because I knew that I was never coming back to them.

## Ghassan, artist (Khan al-Shih camp)

In 1948, my grandfather left Palestine. The family settled in the Golan Heights and started over from zero. In 1967, Israel entered the Golan; we had to leave and again started over from zero. We eventually moved to the Khan al-Shih camp, because it's a poor area and we could afford to buy land and build a house.

I dropped out of school when I was in eleventh grade. I'd always loved calligraphy and drawing. I first worked as a tailor and then in advertising and graphic design. Over ten years, I built a business. It succeeded, and I reached the point where I could go back to school. I finished high school and began studying at the Fine Arts Academy. That was 2011; I was thirty-eight and had four children.

Khan al-Shih became besieged, and the FSA started using the area as a base for its operations. The regime bombed civilians to get them to force the FSA to leave. There was a huge battle and I got displaced from my wife and kids. For a while I lived in a house with twenty-eight other people.

Time passed. I kept hoping that the regime would fall this month, or the month after, or the month after that. My brothers went to Germany, but I didn't want to leave. I felt like I couldn't go to Europe and start over. The things that I'd achieved in Syria might not have been great, but for me they were huge. I'd built a business. I had my name, my reputation, my dream of an education. Leaving Syria meant losing everything and starting from zero, yet again.

I finished my first year at Fine Arts. My wife and children managed to join me in an area where I'd started renting an apartment. My kids looked so much older than when I'd last seen them. At a certain age, a year makes a big difference. My son was twelve, and he'd gotten very tall.

Months went by. Design requires you to do a lot of work from home, but I couldn't, because we had no electricity. I took leave from university, sold my car, and bought a different one that I could use as a taxi. My business had stopped, and work as a taxi driver was steadier.

I enrolled my kids in a new school and would drive them there in the taxi. Every kilometer there was a regime checkpoint. Once, the soldier stopped and asked for my son's ID. I said, "He's only twelve." The soldier said, "Really?" I showed him a note from school proving his age.

This happened another three times. They were paying a lot of attention to age, as they wanted to know if boys were old enough to do their mandatory army service. I thought, "What if he gets stopped at a checkpoint sometime when I'm not with him? They'll never believe that he's twelve." I was scared that they'd take him. That was my nightmare.

I decided that we needed to leave. I'd wanted to stay in

Syria because of what I'd achieved. But that would be self-ish. I couldn't take risks with my kids' futures. When I sold all the equipment in my office, I felt like I was selling a part of myself. The only thing I kept from Syria was my paint-brushes and pens.

# Um Khaled, mother (Aleppo)

Our house was bombed and collapsed on top of us. We spent a year going from place to place inside Syria. We spent all the money we had. First we went to the country-side. We were thirty-five people in one house. The women would sleep in one room and the men in another. When there was shelling, we'd be about three hundred people in the underground shelter.

My youngest daughter, Hayat, was in first grade. She'd wake up at night screaming and her father would hold her. Finally he told me, "You can't bear any more of this. It will destroy you. I want to get you to another country."

I said, "Come with us."

He said, "No, I want to get you to safety." He wanted to stay because our eldest daughter was staying. She is married and has four kids.

So we left and came to Lebanon and my husband and daughter stayed in Syria. I'd talk to him and tell him to get out. He'd say, "You still have a daughter in Syria and I want to be able to check on her. Your siblings and my siblings and their children are also here. I won't leave. The important thing is that I am reassured about you." He'd ask me if I was well and I would say yes. But I was not well. I just wanted to put his heart at ease.

We found a storage space where we could live. I had some gold and I sold part of it to pay the rent. The space had no water, no electricity, nothing. But it was a place for us to sleep—me and my children, my grandchildren, and one of my sons-in-law, who was sick with liver disease. I'm a housewife and have no experience working. But I found work in a factory and worked for six months. I didn't tell my husband.

Then I got news that a plane dropped a bomb and killed seven people. My husband was among them. I don't know if he was inside the house or outside the house. The house was blown away. I tried to get information, to understand what happened. People told me that he was just like everyone else: you're in the street and a missile comes, or who knows what. They sent me a photo of his burial so I'd believe that he was dead.

That was three years ago. When he died, I had to observe a period of mourning, as our religion expects. So I stopped working and stayed home. We had no food or drink. I got my other daughters here from Syria, God knows how. One was eight months pregnant. Her husband was not allowed through. She suffered. She'd faint when she stood up. I'd cry thinking that she was going to die.

I found another job, washing stairs in buildings and sweeping garages. By then we were eighteen people sleeping in the storage space: my four married daughters, my three sons-in-law, their nine children, Hayat, and me. In winter I'd put a thin comforter on the floor for the kids and fold it over them. After they woke up, I'd put it on myself.

Hayat would wake up in the middle of the night screaming, "Mama, they killed Daddy!"

I'd say, "It's okay, God rest his soul."

The other kids would say, "Grandma, look at the mouse!"

I'd say, "It's okay, it won't do anything."

## Safa, mother (Homs)

In Homs, there was no security anymore. The siege never stopped, shooting never stopped. There was no bread, no water, no electricity . . . it became unlivable.

Thank God, we came here to Lebanon. But life is terrible here, too. This neighborhood of shacks, the lack of hygiene, the germs making the kids sick. Whenever it rains, the metal roof leaks. The heater puffs and fills the house with debris. Tap water is so polluted you can't even use it to wash vegetables. My son developed an allergy from the filth. My husband's ears got infected and loads of pus dripped out. And the bugs! In the summer, we have all kinds of insects.

In this neighborhood, all the houses belong to one land-lord. The landlords manipulate rents as they please. At first, our rent was about $230. The bathroom was disgusting. There was no kitchen. I spent all of my savings fixing up the house. Then because of the improvements I'd made, the landlord increased the rent to $300! They tell us, "If you don't like it, go live on the streets."

Everyone takes advantage of Syrians. If you go to the hospital, they register your visit even when they don't provide treatment, just so they can charge the fees to the UN. They cash in and complain about Syrians at the same time. There are organizations that distribute some donations to people, but hoard the rest. Once Kuwait sent clothes; I swear to God that the organizations took the clothes and distributed worn-out secondhand clothes instead. Then Syrians fight each other over the donations, and Lebanese make a fuss that the donations should go to them.

Lebanese won't accept to be paid less than $20 a day, so bosses fire them and hire a Syrian for $10. That leads to tension between poor Lebanese and poor Syrians. We managed to get my husband work selling coffee on the street. He leaves the house at four in the morning and roams around looking for customers. If he stops anywhere, the Lebanese tell him to leave. He can't stay put in any location for long.

My brother is the concierge of a building. They don't give him a salary, just a room to stay in. He had a motor-cycle, but it was stolen. The owner recognized the thieves as guys from the neighborhood. My brother went to file charges, and the police told him, "Take it as advice from us: don't bother. Nothing will come of it, and they might even accuse you of something instead."

The UN used to provide about $30 per person. Then they announced that they ran out of funding. One woman had little children and wanted to register for assistance. They kept telling her to wait. It was such a humiliation; they would leave her to wait for hours in the sun. They'd say "Tomorrow," or "The day after tomorrow." Finally she poured fuel on herself and set herself on fire—right there, outside the UN building.

There's nothing to protect us. No state, no government, no law, no human rights. Animals have more rights than we do.

# Bushra, mother (al-Tel)

Today, kids don't think about going to school in order to be able get a job someday. It's the opposite: They think about getting a job in the hope they will be able to go to school someday. Kids' biggest dream is that they find some sort of work. Or they dream about living in a real house. Sometimes I go to a women's center. One day I took my young daughter with me. She was so excited. After living in a tent, she was amazed by the real walls and real floors. She said, "Take a photo of me next to the wall!"

# Abdel-Aziz, teacher (rural Daraa)

For Jordan, Zaatari is a dead area. They found a place in the desert where not even a tree or an animal can live, and they put the Syrian people there. The other day we saw a butterfly in the camp. Everyone got so excited, we were all shouting at each other to come and look at it. It must have really lost its way if it wound up here.

# Eyad, graduate (Daraya)

Living in Egypt was hard. We were alive, but not really living. My bosses would curse and insult me. Finally I quit my job.

Seven months after we arrived in Egypt, a friend told me that a man we knew was smuggling people to Europe by boat. I thought it was like a joke, but it turned out to be quite serious. It cost about $4,000 per person. In Egypt, that's a full year's salary or more.

My friends and I asked around for money, but only two managed to piece together enough. When they arrived in Europe, I felt envious. I wished that I'd gone, too.

Three months later, another friend asked if I wanted to go. This time, I had the money. We were ten young men and talked to the smuggler. He said, "If you guys get shot and killed, I can't help you. But if you don't arrive in Italy after twenty days, I'll give you your money back."

We packed our stuff and waited. One day the smuggler called and said, "Come now, a bus is ready to take you." I said goodbye to my brothers and sisters. My sister cried, "For God's sake, don't go." I said, "I'm leaving, and that's final." She continued to beg me to stay. Finally, I threw down my bag. I told my friends that I wasn't joining them.

They went. There was a storm and one of them hit his

head and was in a coma for five days. It was a very hard journey, but they arrived. I thought to myself, "Maybe I should have gone, too."

The third time I thought about going to Europe, a friend suggested we go through Libya, which was faster and cheaper. I told my family that I wanted to travel. By then, we'd been in Egypt for fourteen months. My whole family told me to go. No one was crying anymore.

# Maher, teacher (rural Hama)

I was able to defer military service as long as I was enrolled as a student. But then I couldn't afford to pay for my master's program anymore and had to drop out. I no longer had an excuse to keep avoiding the army. I was given a grace period of one month, and so I began to plan my journey from Syria. My friends and I got online and searched for smuggling opportunities from Morocco, Algeria, Sudan . . . We found lists of phone numbers for smugglers, communicated with a few people, and decided to go through Sudan. That was the only country in the world where Syrians were free to visit with only a passport.

The man who drove me to the Damascus airport told me that everyone there was an intelligence officer, even the cleaning people. He warned me that if someone tried to chat with me, I shouldn't talk.

I waited until they called my flight. The agent looked through my passport and found a piece of paper. On one side it said, "Be careful." On the other side it said, "I love you." It was a note from my wife—I didn't know it was there.

He looked at it suspiciously. I said nervously, "My wife. You know how women think."

He answered, "I assure you, if it wasn't for the sentence 'I love you,' you'd be in a lot of trouble." Then he let me proceed.

I arrived in Sudan and I swear it was the first day in five years that I felt safe. I was no longer concerned about checkpoints or police raiding my house.

The smuggler refused to move until we paid him. It was $3,500 to get to the shore and another $500 to cross the Mediterranean. We took Jeeps across the Sudanese desert and then to the Egyptian desert, and then the Libyan desert. Sometimes the car would get stuck in the sand and we'd get out and push. Nobody shot at us, but the Egyptian army shot at cars that left after us, and two people died.

Our boat had about 180 people aboard. The lower deck was all people from Africa and the top deck all Syrians. They told us that we should head toward a star in the sky. The Libyan smuggler left and a young Tunisian took charge of the boat. Then the Tunisian left, too. He told us, "You guys need to take care of yourselves."

# Sadik, veterinary assistant (rural Suwayda)

There were over forty of us in an inflatable boat built for ten. We had to board very quickly, because the Turkish coast guard was on patrol. We helped the women and kids board first. You had to remain sitting in the same position in which you entered, because there was no space to move around.

On the boat we found ourselves to be Syrians, loving each other and caring for each other, even though we're all from different parts of the country. I'm from Suwayda and I was sitting next to a mother and her three kids from Zabadani. The father got stuck on the other end of the boat and there was no way he could move closer to us. I held the kids during the journey and was responsible for their safety. We were all Syrians; all one family.

# Nabil, musician (Damascus)

Al-Jazeera leaked 93,000 names of people wanted by the secret police. I was on it. I needed to leave Syria as fast as possible, but couldn't leave until I got my wife out. She was an extremely accomplished student, someone who had excelled in school her whole life. I wanted to make sure her future was secure.

We searched for scholarships and found one for her to do a doctorate in geology in Portugal. I spent the next fourteen months in Lebanon and Turkey, performing as a musician as I applied for visas to follow her. Nothing worked, so I finally decided to go by sea.

For two years, before I left, I read about what to expect: what to bring, where to go, how to speak with smugglers, how to sleep in a hotel, how to put your phone in a nylon bag for the ride on the dinghy . . . people traveled and then talked about their experiences in detail on the Internet so others could benefit.

For all countries in Europe, you can know the quality of housing, the legal situation, how long you can expect to live in a camp, the duration of your residency permit, etcetera. If someone wants citizenship quickly, he goes to Sweden. For young people who like to have fun, the Netherlands is the choice. Germany is for people who want to study and work. Countries in southern Europe are welcoming and their culture is closer to Syrian culture. But they have economic problems and are still coping with older waves of immigration.

After two or three years of people making these journeys, there's no piece of information you can't find.

# Nur, beautician (Aleppo)

After two years in Lebanon, my husband's work came to a halt. We went back to Aleppo, but found things were even worse then we'd left them. We needed to find somewhere else to go.

We left for Turkey and then made it to the shore. I'd carefully packed one bag with basic necessities: our papers, passports, water, aspirin, rubbing alcohol, toothpaste, a change of clothes, and cookies for the kids. The smuggler told us that there was no room, and we'd have to leave everything behind.

The dinghy arrived. Getting on was like throwing yourself into a deep, dark hole. My husband looked at me and said, "Should we go back?" I responded, "To where?"

In Greece we started walking. My husband carried our son the entire three-week journey. I held our daughter by the hand. We went from Greece to Macedonia, and then to Serbia, Hungary, and Austria before reaching Germany. Everyone along the way tried to make profits at our expense. Days were flaming hot and nights as cold as ice. My feet bled and all I wanted to do was sleep. Every step we took, we found ourselves longing for the one we'd just taken. When we slept on the street, we'd say, "How beautiful the dinghy was." Then we'd get to a field where thousands of people were waiting for days to cross the border from one country to another. We'd say, "How beautiful it was to sleep in the street." But once we started, we couldn't go back. It's as if we were walking on a thread that kept getting cut behind us as we moved forward. Like in the cartoons, when characters cross a bridge that crumbles beneath them as they run.

Once while I was waiting for an appointment in one of the state agencies here I met a journalist. She told me, "The most important thing is that now you're safe." I told her, "But we haven't come looking for safety. We're not afraid of death."

And it's true. We don't have a problem with death. Our problem is life without dignity. If we'd known what was in store for us, we never would have come. But we did come, and now we can't just return. There's no way back.

## Yusra, mother (Aleppo)

I never went to school, so I didn't learn to read or write. I was married at age fifteen and had a son. Then my husband got cancer and died. I had no money, so my son left school and started to work when he was ten. When our problems became too much, he told me, "Mom, you should get married." But whenever anyone proposed to me, he'd say, "This person isn't good for you. I know by looking into his eyes."

Then one day, a man came looking for me. My son talked to him for a while and brought him home. He said, "Mom, I have someone to marry you. I know he's a good man because I looked into his eyes and found kindness." After we got married, my son told me that he wanted only one thing: siblings. He said, "I want a family. I don't want to be alone."

I had a daughter and a son. They were four and two years old when the events began. People started to go out in demonstrations, and then the shooting started. We told ourselves that it would only last a little while. But then came the bombing. When my two-year-old would hear the sounds of explosions, he'd go completely still. He just stared with his eyes wide open, frozen like a tree. It took him a long time to learn to talk. Until he was four years old, he'd say only "bah" and "mah."

I was very scared for my kids, so we smuggled ourselves to Jordan. We took a car part of the way, and then walked in the middle of the night. We paid the FSA to guide us. Whenever the regime army heard a sound, they'd open fire. We thought we were going to die.

We stayed in Jordan for almost two years. Life was hard. There was no work and we spent all the money we had. My husband was still in Damascus. I told him that we needed another solution. He'd worked in Germany in the 1970s and told me, "Germany is beautiful. It's a country that protects the rights of women and children." He had heart problems and high blood pressure, and couldn't make the trip with us. So I told him that I would do it on my own.

I took my two kids and my nephew, and we entered Turkey. There smugglers took us from one place to another. We'd walk up and down hills at night to get to the boats, but the police kept catching us. Once they detained us in a yard under the sun, without a tree for shade. We had no water and my kids got feverish and almost passed out.

I took the kids to Izmir. We kept trying to get on the boat. We'd go, find the police there, and go back. We finally got on a dinghy, and after two hours arrived in Greece. I thought, "That's it. No more struggle, soon we'll be in Germany." I didn't realize that the real journey was only just beginning.

We traveled with a group of about two hundred people. We went by boat to Salonika and then by bus to Macedonia. Then we started to walk. We walked for twenty-nine days. We got lost so many times. Thieves and mafias came out at night and attacked people when they slept, so we'd sleep during the day instead. The young guys would stay awake to guard us. They protected us a lot, but also told me, "You never know what might happen, so you should be strong and get armed." I bought a knife and a big stick.

We entered Montenegro at night and saw police up ahead. The rest of the group wanted to change routes and cross by river. Most of them were young guys and could swim. I was worried that I could lose one of the kids in the dark. I wouldn't put my kids in danger, so I parted ways with the group.

I took the kids and kept walking. Then the police turned their lights on us and shouted, "Police! Police!" I put my knife to my neck and told them, "If anyone comes near me, I'll kill myself!" A woman spoke English and told them what I'd said.

They responded, "We're just trying to protect you from mafias in the area." And that was the truth. The police were good to us. They brought us water and biscuits. They saw that I was dying to rest and let me go to a cave and sleep.

They watched to make sure no one came near us. But after two hours they said I needed to get walking again.

By the time we got to Budapest, my kids were in a terrible state. They couldn't feel anything anymore. Their clothes were wet and they had diarrhea. We finally got to a hotel. I gave the kids a bath and asked them what they wanted to eat. They said chicken, so I went out and got some. We were just starting to eat when someone knocked on the door. It was the police. The hotel owner had reported me.

At the police station they took us from department to department. They insulted us and then put me in one room and my kids in a different room. I cried my eyes out and heard the sound of my kids crying, too.

The next morning they released us and we went back to the hotel. Thank God, we found other Syrians who were leaving that night. We left with them, and eventually made it to Germany.

I've been in Germany for a year and a half now. My husband was able to join us a few months ago. I don't regret a thing. Believe me, if I had to do it all over again, I would. Even if I'm still living in this refugee shelter. God willing, I'll work and live a good life. The most wonderful thing here is the schools. They teach kids until they understand.

I hope that my daughter will be an engineer or a doctor one day. I'm also going to school, and I started to learn the letters. Sometimes I mess up and my daughter laughs at me. But little by little, I'm learning. I learned to ride a bike, too. I fell down so many times in the beginning. But now I'm getting good at it.

## Osama, student (al-Qusayr)

Everything in Jordan bothered me. My family, the government, the bad way the Jordanians treated us. My dad was missing in prison; until now, we don't know anything about him. Personally, I wish that someone would just tell me that he's dead. At least then I wouldn't think about him being tortured.

I was in Jordan for two years and worked a lot of different jobs. People exploited us, because they knew we needed to work to survive. If I quit one job, I might not find another. At the same time, my boss could call the police on me at any moment, because Syrians were legally prohibited from working. They could throw me back to Syria.

If I'd been earning money, at least I could say that I was supporting my family. But the problem was that I wasn't earning much of anything. I enrolled in ninth grade again, because I hadn't finished before we left al-Qusayr. I studied the whole year and took my exams, but they wouldn't give me papers saying that I completed the grade.

I had an uncle in Denmark and told my mom that I wanted to go there to move forward with my life. My brother and I left together. We went to Turkey and agreed with a smuggler to leave on a boat for Italy. We tried two or three times, but the police caught us.

Then another turn came. They threw us on this really small boat. We were 313 people, one on top of the other. It smelled like fish, and everyone was throwing up. Nobody could go to the bathroom and everybody fought over their one glass of water a day. After five days we switched from a metal boat to a wooden one—the kind of boat that tourists take to have a quick swim offshore. We got on and it started sinking. Thank God nobody died.

We were just riding in the water without a clue. The smugglers didn't tell us, but they headed back to Egypt to pick up more people. We were in Egyptian waters when the waves got really strong. The boat almost flipped over. Later, water started to come in from the bottom of the boat. It flowed into the motor and flooded the supply of bread. We took the bread to the roof to dry and it turned all sorts of colors. But we had nothing else to eat.

We moved on to Libyan waters, though we didn't know it at the time. I helped the captain dump buckets of water from the boat so I could get an extra glass of water. The captain liked me and would talk to me. At some point he told me that the boat could take only about six hours more, and then it was going to sink.

By that time you could hear the wood cracking. Everyone started to scream. One guy would pray, others would yell at each other. People started to fight over life vests.

Some people would wear one vest and hide another. It was like the rebels in Syria, stealing from each other. My brother and I didn't wear vests. If the boat sank, people would charge at you and beat you to take the vest. So I thought that I was better off without one. And anyway, if we were going to drown, the vests wouldn't help.

Night came. My brother and I were never really close, but during the trip we became closer than I ever imagined possible. We sat together and he'd hug me tight. We looked at pictures of our family and said goodbye to each other.

Then lights appeared. A boat approached us, yelling, "Italian coast guard!" Everyone started to yell back. It turned out that someone had contacted al-Jazeera and our boat was in the news. We got on the Italian ship. They gave us water. We drank so much, but couldn't quench our thirst. I'd told my mom that the trip would take ten days, but by then, fourteen days had passed. By the time we got to Italy and called our family, they thought we were dead.

In Italy we were placed in a refugee camp, but then managed to escape. We found a Syrian guy who agreed to drive us to Denmark for 500 euros per person. But in Germany our car got pulled over. The driver got like ten years in prison, and we were in jail for two days.

I made it to Denmark. I was in a boarding school for a year, and it was the best year of my life. At first it was hard because I didn't speak the language. But I really wanted to learn, so I started reading and listening to Danish music. Danes won't take the initiative to speak with you; you have to go and talk to them. And that's what I did. I got a Danish girlfriend; she taught me a lot of Danish and now I'm teaching her Arabic. I even visit her family and join them for birthdays and stuff.

I've played piano for years, but only played Arabic music. Here, I've started to play fusions of Western and Eastern music. I play and my girlfriend sings. And it took five years, but I finally finished ninth grade. For five years I was always scared or angry or sad. Then I got a chance to be normal again. I'm happy now. In the end, there's hope.

## Abdul Rahman, engineer (Hama)

I left Hama and went back to Algeria. I got engaged to my love. We were very happy, but in my mind, I was still running and shouting, "Freedom in Syria!" I was spending like ten hours a day reading the news on the Internet, six hours studying, and four hours attending classes at the university. Stress, stress, stress. I got alopecia, a stress reaction disease. I started losing my hair. Later it attacked my eyebrows and eyelashes. Then it started to disfigure my face.

The president of my university knew that I was an activist and he started to close doors on me. He supported the Algerian government, which supported Assad. I was supposed to be admitted to the PhD program automatically because of my high grades. Then, all of a sudden, the department told me that I had to earn admission through an exam like the others. I took the exam and got the second-highest score, but the professors told me, "You're never going to be accepted. Please, just withdraw and give the chance to the student behind you."

I was in shock. I lost my only source of income. My residency in Algeria became illegal. And then I read that Algeria deported nineteen Syrian pro-revolution activists back to Damascus. I told my fiancée and her family that the only solution was for us to get married officially, so at least I had some sort of legal papers in the country. Everybody accepted . . . except my fiancée. Something was wrong. I felt that she had changed. She said that I had changed. Maybe I had.

We got married, but the marriage went downhill quickly. My friends saw my wife with another guy. I confronted her and she said that she was in love with someone else. We divorced, which meant that I lost my residency. I started working in the middle of nowhere in the Algerian desert, because there weren't many police there. Then I got a phone call: My little brother had been killed in an airstrike in Syria. I couldn't handle any more after that.

I got the idea of fleeing to Europe. A Syrian friend came with me. We used smugglers to cross from Algeria to Libya. The smugglers were like an armed gang. They took everything we owned and locked us in a stable for the night. The next day they took us to another smuggler who said what they always say: It will be a very nice boat, with no more than 50 people . . . it turned out to be an old wooden fishing boat about forty meters long, with 350 people on top of each other.

We were at sea for twelve hours before the motor stopped and water started coming into the engine. We started sinking in the middle of the sea. Luckily, the Italian coast guard saw us. They took us onto a big military ship, which was already filled with other immigrants.

In Sicily they asked us if we were educated: engineers, teachers, doctors . . . if you said yes, they took your fingerprints so you stay in Italy. If you said no, they told you to keep moving to northern Europe. My target was Norway, so I told them that I was a laborer.

And so I went—from Milan to Austria to Munich to Hamburg. One train after another. Whenever the police came and checked passports, I'd hide in the toilet. That worked until the German-Danish border, when suddenly the customs police appeared. This very tall guy asked me, "ID, please."

I gave him my expired Syrian passport. He flipped through the pages seriously, looking for a visa or something. He looked at me directly and said, "How did you make it here?"

I gave him a big smile. "By the sea, in a little fishing boat."

He didn't want others to know my issue. He whispered, "Where are you going?"

I said, "Norway."

He gave me back my passport and said, "Good luck." And then he left the train.

I had an aunt in Denmark and stopped to visit her. She

convinced me to stay in Denmark. It took me fifty-one days to be granted asylum. I started my integration plan, which takes three years. I was very serious in language school and then did an online course in computer programming. After two months, I got an internship in an industrial company. All the other interns had been studying for three or four years. I was fully charged with desire to compensate for the years of life I'd lost. I guess it was a way of getting rid of negative feelings of stress and guilt.

Today, I have a job at the biggest IT company in Denmark. My salary is higher than 66 percent of Danes. This company trusted me even though I'm a Syrian refugee with an Arabic, Muslim name. I might have the longest name in the Danish directory.

We have built a Syrian revolutionary community here. The older community of Syrian migrants was too afraid to hold demonstrations. Even in Denmark they said, "Assad supporters will kill us." But we do our demonstrations. Our first one was outside the Russian embassy. We were ten people and the embassy employees treated us like dogs. But we had legal permission and kept going. Our last demonstration attracted at least two hundred people. It was the first of its kind in Copenhagen. I led the chanting, even though I have the ugliest voice in the world. It was so beautiful that I cried. I had the same feeling as when I was in al-Asi Square in Hama.

We want to show that the free Syrian people are out-going, open-minded, successful, and organized. We came from the revolution and we still support our revolution. But I feel guilty. It's not just me. Everybody feels guilty. We talk about it a lot. There were people living peaceful lives and we got them involved in our dream. It was an honest dream, a dream for everybody. But our will—our honest will, our pure will—couldn't make it past international collusions.

Sometimes I dare to think about going back to the revo-lution. But then I remember that it won't make any differ-ence for my country. After I left, my cousin was arrested and killed under torture. Hama today is nearly without men. There are only women and old people. My sister calls it "the Widow City."

# Kareem, doctor (Homs)

Jordanian physicians were worried about competition, so it was impossible for Syrian physicians to get licensed. Instead, we'd work and a Jordanian doctor would claim the work in his name. But the situation was unsustainable. The Ministry of Health heard rumors and began to do inspections. I needed to find an alternative.

I asked around and learned that you could apply for a visa to the United States for only $150. I decided to try. I did the interview and they gave it to me. But then I applied for visas for my wife and children, and their applications were immediately rejected.

I came up with a plan: to book a plane ticket to the U.S. with a layover in Germany, and then get out and stay in Germany. But the airline companies had their own security checks and they refused to approve an itinerary through Europe. Instead I flew directly to New York. I stayed with a Syrian friend for ten days, and during that time consulted with an immigration lawyer. In the U.S., the government basically gives you a work permit and leaves you to fend for yourself. I'd have to study for a long time before I could practice medicine again. During that time I wouldn't earn any money to feed my family.

So I decided to take the other option: Europe. I bought

a ticket from the U.S. to Turkey with a two-hour layover in Frankfurt. In the Frankfurt airport, I waited in a café and kept an eye on my plane to Turkey. They called again and again for a late passenger. Finally, I watched the plane pull away from the gate. When it moved to the runway, I went to the nearest officer, declared that I was Syrian, and requested protection.

A month later I was granted asylum. Within five months my family joined me. I did months of language training and my German is now good, praised be God. At the same time, I was a guest observer at hospitals. I gradually took on more and more responsibilities. About two years after arriving here, I got a contract to work at a hospital. Today I'm a licensed physician again.

I was lucky. But my mind is in turmoil because of the contradiction between the comfort I have here and the suffering of people back home. My conscience bothers me. I'm a doctor; I could have stayed and helped people.

We respect all people and are against all terrorism. But why does this world have such little sympathy for people dying in Syria? A Russian plane is able to drop phosphorus bombs on some human beings because the world has grown accustomed to their deaths. It's as if the blood that circulates in our veins is of lesser value. We've seen only cowardice from the so-called "Friends of Syria." The truth is that Syria has no friends. It is just a chessboard for great powers to settle their accounts.

Our family is scattered. My parents and one of my brothers are in Qatar. Another brother is in Egypt. My other brother was a dentist in Syria. He was desperate to leave because he was about to get drafted into the army. The German embassy rejected his visa application, so he left by sea.

My son spent the first years of his life in Homs stuck inside because of the curfew and the bombing. He had no contact with anyone but his parents and grandparents. He was two years old when he saw another child for the first time. He went up to him and touched his eyes, because he thought that he was a doll.

## Ghayth, former student (Aleppo)

Most Syrians have had to start their lives over at least twice. Someone goes to Egypt and creates a new life, and then *boom!* The political situation changes and he has to leave. He goes to Turkey and gets ruined again and then goes to Greece and gets ruined, and so on.

Germany opened its borders and huge numbers of people came in. I came with that wave. The amount of bureaucracy was unbelievable. Every day I would go to the LaGeSo and wait from seven o'clock to four o'clock.* They did not assign people numbers, so people would sleep outside overnight to hold their spot in line. It took me forty days even to enter the building. I got a number, and then it took another thirty days for my number to show up on the screen. There was no organization. You have number 80 and I have number 90, but number 100 might get called before us. Every day I had to show up, just to see if my number was called. I kept asking them why it never was. Then they discovered that they'd lost my file.

One of the reasons the paperwork takes so long is that

---

* The LaGeSo is the State Office for Health and Social Affairs, where new refugees are required to register upon arrival in Berlin.

many migrants who aren't Syrian claim to be Syrian, because they think we get priority. When I was making the journey, I'd help with translations. I remember watching an Iraqi speak to the Greek police:

"Where are you from?"

"Syria."

"From which city?"

"Mosul."

The police would say, "Mosul is in Iraq."

Now they investigate to make sure that you're really Syrian. They ask you what street you lived on and where you bought your groceries. The employee will pull out a GPS and ask, "How long does it take to walk from Point A to Point B in Aleppo?"

## Imad, former student (Salamiyah)

Everyone was saying, "Just leave, leave, leave." So I left, like everyone else. I didn't even know where I was going until halfway through the journey. I simply moved along with the crowd.

The trip took a month and a half. I was thrown in jail in Hungary, but it was like a five-star hotel compared to my time in our jails in Syria. And by that time I only wanted a break from walking and somewhere warm to sleep.

I don't have any dreams or plans for the future. I hardly think an hour ahead. Return to college? After all those years that I studied and then the revolution started and I couldn't finish and get my degree? I don't have the patience to start again. Besides, even people who have degrees find them worthless once they get here.

Media has tied the revolution to terrorism. If a Syrian asking for asylum says he was with the revolution, European authorities ask for details: Did you see any killing? Did you interact with any terrorists? Who? You feel like you're being accused of something. People just want to get their residency cards. They're afraid of getting sent back. It's easier to say that you're simply running away from war. It's easier not to mention the revolution, or even the regime.

And in this way, the truth of the revolution gets buried. It's getting lost, without our intention or without us even knowing that we're doing it. And that alone is a crime against everything that has happened in Syria.

# Hakem, engineer and pharmacist (Deir ez-Zor)

ISIS started to establish ministries and asked people with university degrees to work with them. I refused. They arrested me for seven days and then released me with a summons to come before their executive court. Everyone knows what that means. I fled to Turkey that night.

It was very hard to leave. I'd been married for one year and my wife was pregnant. After I left, ISIS sent a message to my family telling them that they'd find me in Turkey and finish me off. We know that ISIS can reach into Turkey to take revenge. They also said that they would punish my wife in my place.

I managed to get my wife from Deir ez-Zor to the north of Aleppo, where she hid with her mother. Our daughter was born three months after I left. She is seven months old now, and I still haven't seen her. They are stuck on the border between Turkey and Syria. The Turks have stopped giving residency to Syrians, so the only way to enter Turkey is through smuggling. The soldiers shoot Syrians who try to cross the border.

I have a degree in engineering and twelve years of experience as a pharmacist. Now I'm just sitting here in this refugee shelter doing nothing. My life consists of smoking and drinking tea. All we do is wait. In the evening, you'll see all the people listening to the news on their cell phones. The next day we wake up and wait again. Every day we hear the same news of death. The only difference is the numbers who die.

If I'd known this was life here I would have stayed in Syria and handed myself over to ISIS. It's better to die once than die slowly every day. We're trying to forget our tragedy. But how can you forget your wife or your child or your family? Before I got here, the only time in my life I'd cried was when my father died. Now I cry every day.

## Wael, graduate (Daraya)

I paid a smuggler to hide in a truck from Turkey to Greece. There were four of us and we all lay flat in a narrow compartment like a coffin. The ceiling was less than an arm's length above my face. On one side was a curtain separating us from the driver. On the other side there was a wall. It was so tight that you could only move when the person across from you did. And it was so hot that when I got out I was drenched with sweat. If we ever talked, the driver would yell at us to be quiet. Whenever a border guard stopped the truck to check its papers, we couldn't make any sound at all.

The smugglers told us that the journey would take twenty hours. In the end it took forty. When they dropped us off, we had no idea where we were. I charged my phone and saw that we were close to the border of Sweden.

Sweden is everything I used to dream of for Syria, in terms of how people are treated. It's like people want to make things easier for you, not harder. In Syria, if you wanted to do anything, you have to pay a bribe. Here, you will never have to pay for something that should be your right. If you work hard, you can reach the highest positions of government. All that matters are your qualifications and capabilities. Here you might even see the king filling his car up with gas or buying groceries. It's a long way from the thinking that they implanted in us in Syria—that Bashar was like a god.

The town I live in has only about 60,000 residents, but it has a huge library. It's like a dream. They have any book you want, and if they don't have it, they'll get it from another library. The first time I checked out a book, I thought of Daraya, which had a population of 250,000–300,000 without a single library. That's one of a dictator's strategies: to keep the population in ignorance. A library means people will read, which means they'll think, which means they'll know their rights.

Once my wife and I were walking down the street. An old lady saw my wife's headscarf and said, "Why are you wearing that? Go back to your country!" This bothered us, but we said, "Okay, thank you." We kept seeing her on the same street, so we started taking other streets, instead. We're not here to make problems. But her behavior is racist. It's none of her business what someone else is wearing. On that, the law is on our side.

During my first month in Sweden, I lost my temporary ID card. They told me, "It's no problem. Just go to the police and file a report."

I heard "police" and put one foot forward and another back. I remembered how I had lost my ID card once in

Syria and thought, "Is the same thing that happened there going to happen here?"

I went to the police station. I was really nervous, waiting for them to give me a lot of trouble. But the employee said, "Hello, welcome, what would you like to drink?" I told him about the lost ID. He asked me for my name and where I thought I lost it, and then said, "Okay, thank you."

I asked, "Is that it?"

He said yes. I told him about what happened in Syria when I lost my ID. He said, "I'm very sorry to hear that, but this is all we need from you. If you want to talk about it some more, however, please feel free."

I wish Syria had 10 percent of the democratic system that they have here. If we did, there wouldn't have been a revolution.

## Lana, nuclear engineer (Damascus)

As a teenager, I was always running away from the typical Syrian girl identity. My mom comes from a Christian family and my dad from a Muslim family. They were both very open. But still, they expected me to be gentle, soft, feminine, obedient. Women in Damascus who saw themselves as high class wouldn't go to a café without their hair done, full makeup, and heels. Even in my family, every girl had a nose job.

I rebelled against all of this. I listened to Metallica all day. For seven years, I wore only black. I was always struggling with my dad. I exhausted him: when I went out, when I was late, when I got my lip pierced. At the same time, I got really good grades, especially in physics. Girls didn't usually study physics. But I wanted to piss my parents off.

When I heard about a program in Jordan to study nuclear engineering, I knew that's what I wanted to do. I fought with my dad, hardcore. He didn't want me to go. I would be a girl alone, what would people say? My dad told me that if I went, he'd never be happy with me. He used this expression, which is something like, "I will have a grudge against you forever."

I went anyway. My parents thought, "A nuclear engineer?

No groom will ever come for her now." They gave up. Later, my younger sister followed me to study in Jordan, too.

That was 2008. I used to go back to Damascus every two weeks. On the border, the Jordanian guards respected me. For them, coming from Damascus was like coming from Switzerland. Then after 2011, huge numbers of Syrians started coming in as refugees. The border guards' attitudes changed. They'd yell, "Get out and stand there with the other Syrians."

It was humiliating. Syrians were treated like a burden. By the time I finished university in 2013, I was scared shitless to stay in the Arab world. I needed to run away, anywhere. I applied to graduate programs in more than a hundred universities. Italy, the U.S., Canada . . . every university rejected me. A Syrian working in a nuclear facility? It wasn't allowed.

Then I got accepted to a university in Germany. I went to the embassy for my visa interview and stood outside, crying. I wanted to get out so badly. I'd never wanted anything more.

I got the visa. I finished my master's in two years and submitted 260 applications for jobs. I did twelve interviews; they all loved me but, given all the security checks, it was just too much effort to hire me. Once I took a train eight hours for an interview. When they told me I got the job, I felt like my heart burst. Then they asked for my passport, saying, "You're Jordanian, right?" I took the train eight hours back, devastated.

Finally I got the job I have now. I'm still new, so I do mostly technical stuff, like writing code and making calculations that can prepare reactors should something happen to a pump or generator. Here in Germany they respect that I'm strong and independent. But I've also realized how Syrian I am. The way I enjoy human interaction, the way I let people into my life—this is our Syrian, our Arab culture.

My closest friends here are Syrians I never would have crossed paths with in Syria. One is an amazing guy from this small religious community, the Ibrahimis. Another wrote a book in German. Another is a gay guy, who is the best belly dancer you'll ever see. We're crazy personalities: a collection of new faces and new diseases coming out of war. Some are great minds exploring new possibilities. Some are people who worked in the revolution and are destroyed now. Many have become seriously depressed or are using drugs to cope. They've lost faith in everything.

My friends and I are all sad from the inside, but we never talk about it. We have an understanding: If you want to bring up the war, then do something about it. Go to a protest, take action. If not, just keep your mouth shut. It's like schizophrenia, but it's also a mature way that we've

developed to deal with things. We're all searching for stability. We're trying to live.

You know, if I hadn't gone away for college, I never would
have finished school or gotten where I am today. Even my
dad, who is more hardheaded than I am, recognized this.
He's not the type to express emotion or say, "I love you."
But once, after the war started, he called me and managed
to say: "Thank you for being so stubborn. You saved yourself, and you saved your sister, too."

# Yasmine, education expert (Yarmouk camp)

We said goodbye to our country. I was not going to return until it became a homeland for me again.

What is a homeland? It's not rocks or trees. It's the humans who build the land. It is where you feel safe.

A homeland is a friend with whom you work and drink coffee every morning. And that friend betrayed me for a little money or a better position. As the war intensified, people started reporting each other to the security forces. If anyone held a grudge or wanted revenge on someone, he'd simply file a report about him. And a work colleague filed a report about me. I went for interrogation and they saw that I hadn't done a thing. But you didn't know what might happen the next time they called you in.

I didn't betray my homeland. It betrayed me. It pushed me to leave. When the revolution on corruption turned into a worldwide war, I couldn't consider it a homeland anymore. It became a grave where you die slowly. In my country, I fulfilled my duties, but didn't receive my rights. Here in Sweden, I fulfill my duties and get rights in return. This is what homeland means.

My three children have become holders of European nationalities. My eldest son got an invitation to a convention in Sweden. He stayed and is now in his third year in university. My middle child was invited by a Spanish friend to go to Spain. He became a Spanish citizen and is studying there. My daughter got a scholarship to get her master's in Qatar. From Qatar, she could travel on a tourist visa. She chose to go to Holland and is settling down there now.

In the future, I will have grandchildren who speak Dutch, Swedish, and Spanish. If they don't learn Arabic, they will be strangers to each other. They won't have any traces of where we came from. They won't be Syrian. And I will live in exile and die in exile.

# Iman, engineer (Harasta)

A month after we got to Turkey we registered with the United Nations to be considered for migration elsewhere. The interviewing and security vetting lasted two years.

They asked us about everything that ever happened to us, getting every detail of our lives with complete accuracy. They'd interview my husband and me in two separate rooms. It was a lot of psychological pressure. We were really afraid that we might forget and say different things, especially when it came to dates. Most of us don't remember dates so precisely. My husband said that we fled our house at the beginning of July, but I remembered it as the end of July, which was when shelling had become daily.

After the interviews came the waiting period. I was on the edge of my nerves. You didn't know if you were going to have a future or not. I have a degree in engineering but might never work in my field again. In Turkey, I was lucky to find work in a refugee organization teaching kids how to use computers. Most people didn't find work at all.

For two years, we were living on hope. Every day I'd watch my phone, waiting for the call. My husband is a physician and he ran a small clinic out of our home. He kept waiting for the call, too. And then one day they called. The man told me, "Your trip to the United States is scheduled for September 23." I was in such disbelief, I didn't even understand what he was talking about.

It was really hard in the U.S. at first. Everything was different. The caseworker would speak to me and I would tear up because I couldn't understand what she was saying. Within two weeks I registered for English classes. I wanted to learn so badly, I studied day and night.

I still dream of going back to Syria. We had just gotten married and lived only two months in our new home before we had to abandon it. I'd chosen everything in the house with such care: the furniture, the curtains, the colors of the walls. I dream that I'll go back to it again someday. My husband doesn't want to go back. He has a right to think that way, after what he suffered in prison. For those who suffered like that, it's a blessing to forget.

# Ahmed, activist (Daraa)

We registered as a nonprofit to send supplies from Jordan into Syria. By fall 2014 I was really exhausted. The Syrian regime was threatening to attack me inside Jordan. I already had a visa to the United States, so my wife and I decided to see if we could live there.

Our first trip was supposed to be from Amman to Istanbul to Washington, D.C. They stopped me in the Istanbul airport and sent me back, saying that the Syrian regime had filed a report on me through Interpol. Then I tried to fly directly from Amman to New York, but faced the same issues. The third time, the U.S. embassy gave me a waiver visa. My wife and I finally got to Virginia, where I already had family living.

I immediately applied for asylum. That was like eighteen months ago and I'm still waiting on my application. No response. Just waiting. My wife at least got a number showing that her application was received. She got authorization to work and found a job in her field, graphic and website design. But I haven't received anything. I sent all my information three times. But no response. I'm just stuck here. No passport to return. No authorization to start working. Just stuck. My status is nothing.

Since the last election, we think, "Now what?" Everyone is scared. People are thinking, "If they kick us out, where will we go?" We've started hearing about people being left nasty messages on their doors. Things like "If you're Muslim, leave this neighborhood." My friend has been living in West Virginia for more than five years. His wife has worn a headscarf her whole adult life, but now has decided to stop wearing it. She was very sad but, in this environment, felt like she had to take it off.

The worst part is that people ran away from their own countries because they were being threatened. They come to the United States to feel free, to feel democracy, to feel like they can achieve anything. Now their vision of the United States has changed.

But still, I love this country. So far, my wife and I haven't faced any problems. We hope that won't change. I've actually been amazed by how nice people are. You walk down the street and people just start talking with you about how their husband or wife did this or that. I love that. It's just like back home in Daraa.

In the beginning, some things seemed very complicated for us. In our country, everybody works with cash. In America, we started to learn about debit cards, credit cards, credit history, credit scores. Another thing that was new to us was when you go to a store and they ask for your email and then start sending you advertisements. Like thousands of emails from Home Depot, my God.

Early after I arrived, I rented a car. I drove to a green light and turned left. A police officer stopped me. I said, "But the light was green." He explained that I needed to wait for the arrow signal. I had no idea. We don't have arrows on our traffic lights in Syria.

So now I'm always waiting for the arrow. The guy behind me might be honking and honking. But I will wait for the arrow.

## Hadia, therapist (Damascus)

Twelve of us Fulbrighters from Syria came to the U.S. in 2010. No one had any intention of staying. We were happy to have this opportunity and then go back home.

And then the revolution began. I tried very, very hard to get all the details I could from my cousins and my brother, who were in Damascus. I had this thirst to know, so I could pretend that I was living through their stories. Maybe someday it will make sense to me why I wasn't there while all this was happening. At school people kept telling me, "At least you're safe." That word, "safe," drove me crazy. I wanted to scream, "You don't get it! This is a historical moment. I need to be there."

My mom and brother both got visas to visit the U.S. for my graduation. My mom was planning on staying only a month. But while she was here the regime started bombing the Damascus suburbs, just minutes from our home. We kept postponing her return ticket. We never thought that she'd stay this long. As Mom always says, she came with one suitcase and never said goodbye to people.

At that time, my brother was working with a charity bringing food to besieged areas around Damascus. Many of his friends got arrested, because providing bread was like a crime. When one person is arrested, they go through his phone and take everybody else they can. There were only three days left before my brother's U.S. visa expired, so we insisted that he come here, too. When he arrived, you could see in his face that he was a traumatized person. He spent all his time online trying to follow events, connect people, raise money for medical supplies, etcetera.

Winter came and I told my mom, "Lets go shopping and get you a coat."

She said, "I can't believe that I'm going to buy things while people are dying in Syria and have nothing to wear."

I'd say, "We have to. It's Chicago and it's cold."

She'd say, "But I have all those coats in Syria."

It's the small things like that. They become like rocks on your chest and you feel like you need to push through them, one by one. You can't buy a sandwich without thinking, "How much is this sandwich? If this money was sent to Syria, then . . ."

My role is different from people on the inside, but I need to do something. I have a responsibility to tell the story. To talk about what is happening on the other side of the world.

Part VIII

# REFLECTIONS

## Abu Ma'an, activist (Daraa)

We know that freedom has a price. Democracy has a price. But maybe we paid a price that is higher than freedom and higher than democracy. There is always a price for freedom. But not this much.

# Ghayth, former student (Aleppo)

Today, the word "refugee" is used in a horrible way. It's something either to be pitied or blamed for everything. Overpopulation? It's the refugees. Rents going up? It's the refugees. Crime? It's the refugees. If you label people refugees, they remain refugees for the rest of their lives. For that reason, the organization I work with here doesn't use this word. Instead, we say "newcomers." After a while, they are no longer newcomers—just members of society.

As Middle Easterners, we're trying to show people who we really are. I'm not an angel and I'm not a devil. But I will do my duty. I didn't come here to take anything away from you. I want to work with you.

This is what we learned in the revolution. We learned how to play our part. We worked so hard for this revolution, and it was so innocent. And then it turned into a war and everyone got involved in stealing it. Good leaders with good reputations were assassinated. The FSA was reduced to a matter of funding. If the funding was from Qatar, they had to do what Qatar wanted. If the funding was from Turkey, they had to do what Turkey wanted. This happened because the war dragged on and on.

Many people aren't happy with the refugees coming

to their country. Maybe we came illegally, but every other door was shut in our faces. What do they expect us to do? Isn't it enough our government destroyed us and we lost everything? We would prefer to stay in our country. If you don't want refugees, help us make peace in Syria.

# Sami, graduate (Damascus)

My family supports the Assad regime. Especially my mother. She's a true Christian believer who goes to church every Sunday. She loves her country and wants to stay there. I think my mom knows that the regime is oppressive and violates human rights. But at the same time, she has this nightmare that if the regime falls, we're doomed. She thinks, "We know that the regime is bad, but it's protecting us, and we shouldn't criticize it."

I'm also a believer, but I don't think that way. The regime isn't protecting Christians, it's only protecting itself. Assad isn't protecting Alawites, either. He's exploiting Alawites. He's manipulating the issue of minorities. He wants to stay in power and minorities are one of the cards that he can use.

I criticize rebels who kill and I criticize the regime. There was an explosion in my neighborhood and children died. I posted pictures and wrote, "Stop the war." I was showing sympathy toward people who died in an area that does not support the uprising, so my friends who support the uprising saw me as supporting the regime. A few days later, there was the chemical massacre. I posted pictures of the people dying there, too. My friends and family questioned my actions.

I'm not a traitor. I love Syria. But I believe in human rights and I can't feel like I belong to a society that oppresses women or children or people from other ethnic backgrounds. That oppressiveness is a part of Christianity, not just Islam. Arabs used to produce science and algebra and now we're famous for killing. We should take responsibility in order to improve ourselves. If we change the regime but don't change our broader culture, the same regime will come back, just with different people.

# Khalil, defected officer (Deir ez-Zor)

The revolution will not give up. You think I'm going to return to Syria and say that Bashar al-Assad is my president? Impossible.

But personally, I've reached a point of despair. Despair with the opposition leadership, despair with the patron states. The crux of the problem is that every country—Saudi Arabia, Qatar, the UAE, etcetera—is supporting its own group. Many countries have interests in the country, and they're all woven together like threads in a carpet.

We don't know where any of this is leading. All we know is that we're everyone else's killing field. The only way I can understand this is that these other countries don't want the crisis in Syria to end. They want to scare their own people from demanding change. They want to send a message to their own populations: If you make a popular revolution, you're going to wind up like Syria.

Most of the calls I get are from Syrians desperate for aid of one kind or another. What can I tell them? Many times, I don't even answer the phone. There is nothing I can do for them. To be honest, there are times when I wish I could forget everything. There are times when I want to take my wife and kids and go somewhere and just raise my family.

## Marcell, activist (Aleppo)

I belong to the revolution generation and I'm proud of that. We tried our best to build something. We faced a lot, and we faced it alone. And we faced it with the minimum of hatred toward others. But we lost control. We don't know anymore what is useful. Here in Turkey, I work more than ten hours a day, and at end of the day, I wonder, "Did I accomplish anything? Is it going to change anything?"

To me, the revolution is like a child with special needs. I believe in it and can't abandon it. Yeah, it's nothing like I dreamt it would be, and in some places, we're the new dictators. But to me, it's like he's my son and I just should have taken better care of him.

Most us right now are disappointed and depressed. During the first three years, our motive was positive change. For the last three years, our motive has been guilt. Those who are dying are the poorest. You can't lessen their suffering, so you at least want to return to Syria and suffer with them. No one, not even the refugees, can celebrate mere survival. If I make a purpose out of simply surviving, does that mean that my mother died for no reason? That my friends died for no reason?

Syrians aren't really talking about this sense of guilt. They talk about Syria. Syria, Syria, Syria. No one talks about himself or herself. I'm afraid that I'm forgetting who I am. Sometimes I find myself writing "she" when I should be writing "I." As if I'm telling someone else's story.

This year I'm going to try to go somewhere and find some space to become a person again. Right now, my friendships are political, my work is political, my reading is political, my writing is political. I went on a date, and the first question the guy asked me was, "Do you think the opposition will go to the peace talks in Geneva?"

I don't want to be only a political thing. I want to be able to laugh, tell jokes, enjoy music. To be a person with dreams, hopes, love. I have a lot of anger at the world and I want space to heal. I want to find the space to be me.

## Ayham, web developer (Damascus)

I still believe that what we did is right. Sadly, what we did turned out horribly.

I'm not glorifying us, but for me, it's clear that the regime is to blame. If it's the regime's responsibility to protect our national identity, it didn't do that. If it's the regime's responsibility to protect our national interests, it didn't do that. If it's the regime's responsibility to respect our social dissent, it didn't do that, either.

One of the saddest things is that when we were raised to worship the regime we were also fed a certain pride. Pride in our culture, in our name. Like when you said, "I'm Syrian," it carried respect. We work hard. Even the poor enjoyed life. You know, everybody had picnics. They tried to buy decent cars. They gave their kids the chance for education. That was Syrian pride. We grew up singing these Baath Party songs in school. I don't believe the Baath ideology, but some of its ideals were quite nice in principle. "We are farmers and workers, the youth that never breaks. We are the fighting soldier and the voice of those who toil . . ." Even today, when I sit with my friends and sing those songs, I feel like I belong.

# Talia, TV correspondent (Aleppo)

We were living under dictatorship for forty years and we were tired. Tired of hypocrisy. Tired of only getting a job if you have connections. We wanted to know this famous thing called freedom. But now if you sit with one thousand Syrians, they'll each give you their own sense of freedom. Some women ask themselves, "If I take off my headscarf, will I be free? If I change my religion, will I be free?" In my opinion, that's not what freedom is about. For me, freedom is living in a society that respects me. Freedom is being able to express myself. Freedom is the chance to do something for which people will remember me.

In Syria, women were dependent on men. The root of the problem was our failed government. There weren't any laws to protect women. They didn't know their rights or their worth. This changed with the revolution. People no longer had the barrier of fear, and women no longer feared their husbands. Now a woman can say no and say yes. She can rebel.

When I got to Turkey I sat at home for the first year. My mental state was at rock bottom. I had wanted to separate from my husband for years, but I delayed the decision. Then I got stronger and became financially stable. I was living in a country where the law defended me. And so I left him and the house and everything. All I took was my kids. I started again from zero.

I had worked for a few months in radio, and then a job opened at a major TV network. Ten other people applied for it, and they all had degrees in journalism. I didn't, but I wanted the job. For three months, I practiced how to speak before the camera. I'd stand in front of the mirror and talk to myself. I would record my voice and say words this way and that way to figure out how to make them sound better.

I did an interview with the manager. She told me she didn't want to hire me, but that I have a kind of talent that not all journalists have. She said, "Talia, I wish you weren't this good." And, just like that, I got stuck in her head. And I got the job.

I discovered that I'm a person who can have an impact on others. It was the revolution that taught me to be impactful in this way. And it was the revolution that allowed me to see people for who they really are. It showed me that every Syrian has a hundred stories in his heart. Every Syrian is himself a story.

## Adam, media organizer (Latakia)

One of the most profound things that I learned from this experience called the Syrian civil war is this: Just because you're fighting evil doesn't mean you're good. And just because you're doing evil doesn't mean you're bad. You end up with the conclusion that there is no ultimate right or wrong. It's all shades of gray.

The process of finding out what a country needs is never clean. Of course, when you're in a stable country with functioning institutions it's easy to have a moral code. But just keep in mind that these values are only made possible for you because other people did dirty things to put that system in place. People don't want to know about that dirty work because it doesn't fit with their idea of who they are.

I think that's what people mean when they say, "We're fighting for your liberty," or clichés of that sort. As a country, we need somebody to do the wrong thing in order for future generations to have a life that is morally stable and functioning. That way, they won't have to compromise on morality all the time in small ways, like we had to do in Syria.

That's what I've learned from this whole thing called the Syrian war. For us, people who are not privileged enough to have the freedom to be good people, we have to make some bad choices and do some evil things. That's shitty, but it is what it is. Ironically, we went out in demonstrations to eradicate corruption and criminal behavior and evil and hurting people. And we've ended up with results that hurt many more people.

We opened a Pandora's box. We had this innocent, child-like interest to see what was inside the box. We thought we'd get a present, and what we got was all the evil in the world. Now we need to close the box again, but it's going to take a while.

What's crucial in this whole process is that you don't matter. You as an individual—your aspirations, your ideas about what is right—mean absolutely nothing. And that's when you understand why people get radicalized. I completely understand why somebody would join ISIS or al-Qaeda or the Assad regime or the Kurdish groups. You are in dire need for a narrative that can justify this futility. There has to be a point. So you become radical. This suffering has to be for a reason. Otherwise it's too painful.

Now I'm working with an NGO that helps the free media and press inside Syria. I'm trying to help journalists say what they want to say. I see my job as trying to support these people who want to make their dreams come true. But I think I'm too old to dream now. In a month and a half, I'll be twenty-nine.

## Husayn, playwright (Aleppo)

I try not to talk about politics anymore. Things are no longer clear. It's hard to know what's right and what's wrong.

Every time one of my close friends wants to leave for Europe, I don't try to stop him. But it makes me very sad. When someone sells all his belongings and puts his family's lives in danger to travel by sea to Europe, he's unlikely to come back. And if everyone who participated in the dream of a free Syria leaves or gets killed, who is going to build Syria later?

I have hope there are still people inside Syria who want to build it. Half of those living under regime control don't even support the regime. But the conflict doesn't belong to us anymore. Political money and weapons entered the country. Syria has become an arena for other countries to settle scores. Bashar is a puppet in Russia's hands and we are puppets in the other sides' hands. We never expected that these dark groups would come into Syria—the ones that have taken over the game now.

We sometimes ask ourselves, did we help cause all this chaos in Syria? I think that we could have been more organized and better prepared for what was coming. We could have been more careful about timing. I feel sad, but I don't feel regret. I'm proud that I was one of the people who chose change. I believe that we were able to destroy the foundations of tyranny.

Some so-called intellectuals and old politicians stood on the sidelines, waiting to see what was going to happen before they chose a side. Some of them are now gloating. I say to them, "When we joined the revolution, we were strong. If you had stood with us then, we wouldn't be weak now." Other people fighting the regime want an Islamic state. I know that they want to control my life. But we can argue about that later. First we need to bring down the regime.

Our dreams have changed in stages. Our dream before the revolution was different than during the revolution, and it's different now. We've accepted the fact that we need to make our dreams smaller if that's what it takes to keep dreaming.

# Acknowledgments

While many books include long lists of people to thank, this is even more the case for a book of this type. Every word between these covers got here because someone generously shared his or her story with me and someone else kindly introduced me to him or her in the first place. This makes me atypically indebted but also unusually fortunate, as the writing of this book allowed me to meet countless amazing people, many of whom have become lifelong friends.

My greatest debt is to the hundreds of Syrians who selflessly welcomed me into their lives and spoke to me about their thoughts, feelings, and experiences. They taught me the meaning of dignity, commitment, and resilience. Though they are too many to name, I hold each of them in my heart. I am forever changed, and will be forever humbled, by the privilege of having met them.

I am especially grateful to those who went above and beyond connecting me to people to interview, namely Shafiq Abdel-Aziz, Ghaidaa al-Haj, Ahmed Al-Masri,

Salma al-Shami, Maha Atassi, Abdalsamad Awida, Firas Diba, Wa'el Elamam, Hamzah Ghadban, Cherin Hamdoche, Suha Ma'ayeh, the late Tayseer Masalma, Noman Sarhan, Rana Sweis, Hadia Zarzour, the Awida family, Ghadban family, al-Haj family, Sarhan family, Darwazah family, Alobid family, and Radio Shebab team. Their commitment to their ideals is an inspiration and their trust in me nothing less than an honor.

Had I had to transcribe and translate all interviews myself, this book would have taken a decade to finish. Thankfully, I met with skilled assistance from more than twenty translators-transcribers over the years. I give special thanks to Lina Abdelaziz, Jamal Abuzant, Ameer Al-Khudari, Serene Darwish, Nada Sneige Fuleihan, Nadia Mantabli, and Jude Wafai for their work on a heroic number of transcripts. I am grateful to Clara Clymer and Alli Divine for research assistance across different stages of this work and to Rana Khoury, and Ameer Al-Khudari, for reading the manuscript in full.

This book is one harvest from a larger research project on Syria made possible by support from the Project on Middle East Political Science, the Alexander von Humboldt Foundation, and several programs at Northwestern University, namely the Buffett Institute for Global Studies' Equality Development and Globalization Studies Program and Keyman the Modern Turkish Studies Program, the Alice Kaplan Institute for the Humanities, and the Crown Family's support for Middle East Studies. Over four years and four continents, I delivered presentations of this and other works-in-progress on Syria, during the course of which I benefited tremendously from astute feedback. These exchanges directly or indirectly shaped the thinking that went into crafting this book, and for that I owe particular thanks to Marc Lynch, Ellen Lust, Hamisch Cultural Center-Istanbul, the American University of Beirut, Boğaziçi University, George Washington University, Lund University, NYU-Abu Dhabi, Sabancı University, the University of Copenhagen, the University of Denver, the University of Michigan, the University of Washington, and colleagues in the Political Science Department and Middle East and North Africa Studies Program at Northwestern University.

This book would not have come to be without the encouragement, literary vision, and hard work of my agent Ayesha Pande and editor Geoff Shandler. They not only made this a better book, but made me a better writer, as well. The journey was not always easy, and I have been fortunate to count on emotional support from friends and family such as Theo Christov, Raja Halwani, Jana Lipman, Karen Kice, Jen Marlowe, Almas Sayeed, Suzanne Travers, and Marc

VanOverbeke, Judith Schwab, Judy Kolker, Alicia Pearlman, and Charlie Pearlman. My partner, Peter Cole, kept me going with his wisdom, humor, patience, and rock-star vegan cooking, all while he was busy writing his own book, too. I cannot express my love and appreciation for him. My father, Michael Pearlman, has always had my back; I am more grateful for him than he will ever know. My grandmother, Margaret Pearlman, remains my light and moral compass. Her tireless political activism, now well into her nineties, has taught me that there is no higher calling than solidarity with those struggling for freedom and justice.

# ABOUT THE AUTHOR

Wendy Pearlman is a professor and award-winning teacher at Northwestern University, specializing in Middle East politics. Educated at Harvard, Georgetown, and Brown, Pearlman speaks Arabic and has spent more than twenty years studying and living in the Arab World. She is the author of numerous articles and two books, *Occupied Voices: Stories of Everyday Life from the Second Intifada* (Nation Books, 2003) and *Violence, Nonviolence, and the Palestinian National Movement* (Cambridge University Press, 2011). She lives in Chicago.